CHOOSING COLLEGES

CHOOSING COLLEGES

*How Social Class and Schools
Structure Opportunity*

Patricia M. McDonough

STATE UNIVERSITY OF NEW YORK PRESS

Published by
State University of New York Press, Albany

© 1997 State University of New York

For information, address State University of New York Press,
State University Plaza, Albany, N.Y., 12246

Production by Cathleen Collins
Marketing by Fran Keneston

Library of Congress Cataloging-in-Publication Data

McDonough, Patricia M., 1952–
    Choosing colleges : how social class and schools structure
opportunity / Patricia M. McDonough.
        p.   cm.
    Includes bibliographical references and index.
    ISBN 0-7914-3477-X (alk. paper). — ISBN 0-7914-3478-8 (pb : alk.
paper)
    1. College choice—United States.   2. College choice—Social
aspects—United States.   3. Counseling in secondary education—
United States—Case studies.   4. High school students—United
States—Social conditions—Case studies.   I. Title.
LB2350.5.M377   1997
378.1'98—dc21
                                                                    96-47380
                                                                    CIP

10 9 8 7 6 5 4 3 2 1

To equity in college access.

Contents

Tables

Acknowledgments

I am deeply indebted to the students, their families, and the counselors who participated in this study. Without their willingness to let me into their lives and their thinking, this book would not have been possible. Each of them has informed and inspired me.

I would like to give special thanks to Milbrey W. McLaughlin, Joan E. Talbert, W. Richard Scott, and Marshall Smith for their time, suggestions for improvement, and colleagueship. Milbrey, in particular, has been a first-rate mentor, who continues to teach me invaluable lessons about research as well as teaching. James Hearn has been an important colleague who has provided me with encouragement, advice, and suggestions. Megan Franke played a key role in getting this manuscript off the shelf, for which I am indebted. I also appreciate the suggestions of the anonymous reviewers.

I am profoundly appreciative of the help that Deborah J. Hales provided me. But above all, I owe my deepest thanks to Sabina Mayo-Smith, as well as Winifred and William McDonough. All three of you have never wavered in your belief in me and my research, and have given me the love and support necessary to complete this book.

CHAPTER ONE

Who Goes Where to College?

Who goes where to college? This study examines the ways in which social class and high school guidance operations combine to shape a high school student's perception of her opportunities for a college education. It is also an analysis of the intersection of family, friends, and school network effects and how they create individual biography.

The late twentieth century is a time of rapid change in the college admissions world. Given the decline in the number of high school graduates, there should have been a buyer's market in college admissions, but in fact students face intense college access competition. Although it is easier to get into college now than it was twenty years ago, it is harder to get into what some people consider the "right" college (Winerip 1984) because of rising admissions standards and stratification of higher education opportunities. The Harvard Dean of Admissions reported that not only are today's median Scholastic Aptitude Test (SAT) test scores more than 100 points higher than they were in 1950s classes, but over that same time period, Harvard has gone from admitting over 60 percent of applicants to admitting only 15 percent to 20 percent (Fitzsimmons 1991).

Through a complex interactive process involving individual aspiration and institutional admissions, students connect with colleges. Potential students find out about and enroll in college through the encouragement of family, friends, high school advisors, teachers, private counselors, freeway signs, radio, television, newspaper, and direct mail advertising, and many other sources. Colleges, in their admissions processes, go through many stages: marketing assessments, recruitment, establishing admissibility criteria, selection, notification, and enrollment.

Approximately 62 percent of high school seniors (about 2.2 million first-time freshmen) find places annually in approximately 3,600 colleges in the highly stratified U. S. system of postsecondary education (Snyder and Hoffman 1995). This figure suggests an opportunity structure that is fair, open, and meritocratic. In fact, society's opportunity structure does not work equally well for all. The aggregate

1

college enrollment rate masks vast discrepancies in the access and retention rates between white students and students of color, as well as between economically advantaged and disadvantaged students. These differentials in access and attrition in postsecondary education present empirical patterns that inform this research.

This study addresses three questions:

1. How does a high school senior in today's college admissions environment make decisions about where to go to college?
2. How does this decision-making process vary by the student's social class, the social class makeup of the student's high school, and the structure and context for guidance available in the high school?
3. Why, if there is a single opportunity structure for American higher education, do individuals perceive it differently?

Opportunity structures are "the pathways to success in American culture," (Marshall 1994), and I am specifically referring to the organizational arrangements and processes within institutions and the linkages between organizations that define and mediate individuals' achievements. Opportunity refers to prospects for mobility from the individual's present position to higher- and lower-level positions. For high school students who are choosing a college, their academic achievement, class background, and high school's perspective on desirable college destinations will shape how they perceive their higher education opportunities. No one student perceives the opportunity structure in its entirety, but instead, imagines schools that she deems "right" or "appropriate," or schools where she will feel comfortable. In the following section, I review the broad patterns in college access and retention found in prior research and suggest areas needing further inquiry.

Patterns of Educational Attainment

Across all achievement levels, students from the lowest socioeconomic (SES) groups are less likely to apply to or attend college than are the highest SES students. For example, among the highest-ability students, 60 percent of the lowest SES students attended college, while 86 percent of the highest SES students attended (Gardner 1987). Students of color and poor students are less likely to start or finish college (Levine and Nidiffer 1995) and are more likely to attend low prestige colleges or those with the highest dropout rates (Hearn 1984).

To paraphrase Gertrude Stein, A college is not a college is not a college. Researchers and policy experts note the existing organizational stratification within the higher education sector (Trow 1984; Pascarella, Smart, and Stoecker 1989; Smart and Pascarella 1986). There are salient distinctions between two- and four-year colleges (Velez 1985), selective and nonselective universities (Karabel and Astin 1975; Kingston and Lewis 1990), and private and public institutions, which produce important sources of inequality in adult life (Coleman, Rainwater, and McClelland 1978). Where one attends college influences one's eventual educational attainment (Alba and Lavin 1981; Presley 1980; Sewell 1971; Useem and Karabel 1986).

Research also shows that the college one attends significantly affects one's chances of completing the baccalaureate, and that the proportions of students who persist until they graduate vary widely across institutions, even after academic ability is controlled (Velez 1985). Elite institutions have graduation rates of between 85 percent and 95 percent. Four-year public institutions have much lower rates, approximately 45 percent (Snyder 1987). Community colleges, which enroll over half of first-time freshmen, have transfer rates of about 20 percent (Adelman 1988); baccalaureate degree completion rates for those students who begin at community colleges are even lower (Brint and Karabel 1989).

Research evidence indicates that observed college attendance patterns are as much an issue of *self*-selection processes as they are of college admissions decisions. Ninety percent of 1980 seniors included in the High School and Beyond longitudinal sample were admitted to their first-choice institution (Karen 1988). When students apply to college, most use their SAT scores as a self-screening device to identify colleges where they are likely to be accepted and where other students' have similiar SAT scores (Manski and Wise 1983). I now review the major approaches to studying college choice.

College Choice Research

There have been three basic approaches to the study of college choice decision-making influences.

1. *social psychological studies*, which examine the impact of academic program, campus social climate, cost, location, and influence of others on students' choices; students' assessment of their fit with their chosen college; and the cognitive stages of college choice;
2. *economic studies*, which view college choice as an investment decision and assumes that students maximize perceived cost-benefits in their college choices; have perfect information; and are engaged in a process of rational choice; and
3. *sociological status attainment studies*, which analyze the impact of the individual's social status on the development of aspirations for educational attainment and measure inequalities in college access.

The literature tells us that the college-choice process can be a lengthy one that extends back to the earliest inculcation of college aspirations and begins with a broad overview of the postsecondary educational opportunities available to students (Chapman 1981; Hossler, Braxton, and Coopersmith 1989). Passing through a variety of stages, each student narrow her options to a single set of institutions (Hossler and Gallagher 1987; Jackson 1982; Litten 1982). The Hossler model specifies those stages as predisposition, search, and choice. In the *predisposition phase*, a student first decides whether to attend college. The *search phase* occurs when the student searches for general information about colleges, forms a choice set, and begins to consider several specific colleges. In the final *choice phase*, the student winnows the choice set down to a single college and chooses to attend that college.

In students' search and choice phases, a number of factors have been found to be consistently influential: parents; the college's size, location, academic program, reputation, prestige, selectivity, and alumni; the student's peers, friends, and guidance counselor; and availability of financial aid (Hossler, Braxton, and Coopersmith 1989; Manski and Wise 1983; Zemsky and Oedel 1983). Most college choice research focuses on students' background and institutional characteristics. Although this is not a study of institutional influences on college choice, two collegiate institutional factors that affect the college choice process are the kind and amount of financial aid a student receives and the total cost of tuition and expenses (Leslie and Fife 1974; Manski and Wise 1983; St. John 1990), as student aid has been found to result in (1) increased consumption of higher education and (2) a redistribution of students to private, four-year, and smaller institutions.

One feature of college choice research is that it has nearly exclusively been the domain of quantitative analysts. This book will expand on the insights of three decades of college choice research by providing micro-level insights and a finer-grained analysis of how students proceed through their predisposition, search, and choice phases. Specifically, I will examine the processes and influences of students' everyday lived experiences in social class communities and schools and investigate how these influences shape students' college choices. Moreover, this study will integrate the investment, aspiration, and individual-institution fit perspectives of the existing college choice models in a new theoretical approach. Before presenting this approach, I will first review what insights we have gained on college attainment from the existing status attainment and high school context effects literature.

Status Attainment Literature

For all students, academic achievement remains the most important determinant of whether and where they go to college (Alexander and Eckland 1975; Hearn 1991; Karen 1988; and Thomas 1979). However, systematic relationships exist within achievement groupings between income and college selectivity (Hearn 1991). Independent of academic factors, upper-income youth are especially likely to enter America's elite colleges (Hearn 1987). African Americans, women, and low-SES students are especially likely to attend less-selective institutions, even if their ability and achievements are high (Hearn 1984 and 1990).

Students' educational expectations play a major role in college placement (Hearn 1984) and oftentimes are the single strongest predictor of four-year college attendance (Thomas 1980). Long-standing college goals can be resources: intending to go to college increases the likelihood of going by 21 percent when that intention develops prior to tenth grade, compared to plans formulated during the senior year (Alexander and Cook 1979).

Hearn (1984) contends that students' and parents' perceptions, attitudes, and knowledgeability about college attendance may take on distinctive shapes for different social classes and races as early as the tenth grade and thus may produce differences in families' college planning. For example, high SES students tend to take more college preparatory courses.

However, students' educational plans are unstable predictors of actual behavior. Moreover, there are major differences in the application practices of students from different socioeconomic statuses (McDonough 1994): first-generation college-bound students tend to opt for the most competitive Ivy League institutions or less expensive state schools—while middle- and upper-income students apply everywhere (up to twenty-two applications), even though application fees begin at forty dollars.

Multivariate analyses suggest a hierarchy of effects of background characteristics on educational attainment. The order of effects, from strongest to weakest, is social class, race, and gender. Holding achievement constant, race appears to be more influential than gender in affecting the process of college entry (Thomas 1979). For example, survey data suggests that Asian Americans have a strong orientation to selective colleges and are twice as likely to apply to the best schools as white students (Karen 1988). One researcher contends that African Americans and Hispanics, as a group, are not as likely to try to get into highly selective colleges because of their subjective assessments of the impact of their lower grades, test scores, and levels of participation in extracurricular activities (Karen 1988).

The most stubborn barriers to parity in entrance to college, however, are in social class background rather than race, ethnicity, or gender (Hearn 1984 and 1991). Social class status exerts twice as much effect on the selectivity of a student's college choice as does ethnicity or gender (Karen 1988). However, gender seems to be significant largely in interaction with SES. Earlier research showed that the sorting of women into college destinations is much more strongly affected by status origins than it is for men (Alexander and Eckland 1977), while recent research has documented some lessening of gender impacts (Hearn 1991) but also the differential conversation capacity of women's educational assets (Persell, Catsambis, and Cookson 1992). Thus, working class women are more disadvantaged in educational attainment than are their male counterparts.

The substantial impact of class status on educational attainment operates directly through individual choice and indirectly through the impact of scholastic aptitude on available options (Karen 1988). The ways in which SES affects students' choices is mediated, in part, by parents' knowledge of what it takes to prepare for college. For twenty years, large-scale quantitative studies have dominated the educational attainment field, repeatedly demonstrating that the mother's and father's educational attainment, proxy effects like the number of books in the home, and related variables affect a student's attainment. However, this research has been labelled atheoretical because it has not adequately explained *how* or *why* these factors are influential (Knottnerus 1987).

A number of differences exist between low SES, first-generation college-bound students and high SES students whose parents had completed college. Students who are first-generation college-bound begin to think about going to college much later than do students whose parents have gone to college, and those thoughts tend to be triggered by school personnel, specifically teachers and counselors (McDonough 1988). Students whose parents have attended college often get a head start on college preparations in elementary school by taking the right courses and maintaining good grades, and their families convey information to them about the different types of colleges and universities. Meanwhile, first-generation college-bound students do not get this information, oftentimes are not taking the right courses, and are struggling with the cultural conflicts between their new college-oriented world and the world of their friends, families, and communities.

The issue least well-understood about students' college destinations is the causal process—the web of opportunities, structural arrangements, contingencies, and timing—through which school context, SES, and family together shape the process of college planning and choices (Hearn 1990 and 1991). The existing studies of educational attainment emphasize individual attributes as the key determinants of inequalities, largely neglecting the role of educational institutions. In contrast, the broader stratification literature suggests organizational contexts as critical to understanding the empirical patterns of individual educational outcomes.

School Effects Literature

The high school environment has a powerful influence on the ways in which students choose colleges. Only two models of college choice, which are both considerably dated, incorporate high school context effects primarily through the shaping of aspirations. Boyle (1966) suggests that college aspirations are influenced not only by individual ability and motivation but also by the imposition of academic standards and the practices of a college-focused high school. Alwin and Otto (1977) offer further insights by differentially analyzing the individual's ability and socioeconomic status levels and the high school's average ability and socioeconomic status levels.

Yet, as seen in more recent research, public and private schools appear to differ in important ways regarding college enrollment decisions and culture. About half of the difference in the higher college attendance rates of private school students can be accounted for by socioeconomic status for non-Catholic, private school students and by differences in orientations and expectations of parents toward college attendance in Catholic school students (Coleman 1987). Researchers have attributed the balance of college attendance differences to:

- the organization and content of curriculum and extracurricular activities;
- higher academic standards and the value climate;
- formal and informal communication networks;
- orientation of school staff; and
- resources devoted to counseling and advising of college-bound students (Falsey and Heyns 1984; Alexander and Eckland 1977).

Seniors enrolled in private high schools are significantly more likely than public school seniors to enter college and enroll in four-year institutions, even when track, ability levels, aspirations, and SES are controlled (Falsey and Heyns 1984). On average, private schools are smaller, have different rules and expectations, and have larger percentages of students in the academic track than do public schools. Private schools also help students develop their college aspirations better than do public schools through a greater proportion of counselors per student, who encourage and influence a large proportion of their students in their college planning. (Falsey and Heyns 1984; Coleman, Hoffer, and Kilgore 1982).

Research on guidance and counseling indicates that a school, public or private, can affect college plans through an ethos of enabling students. This ethos should be held and acted upon by knowledgeable staff who affect students in daily interactions even without directly exposing students to specific college preparatory programs (Hotchkiss and Vetter 1987). The disparity of organizational mission and resources between public and private schools necessarily has an impact on students' planning for college. In summary, having college plans at least by the tenth grade, attending a college-focused high school, having parents who expect their children to go to college, and having assistance in negotiating an adequate financial aid package are the key determinants to college attendance and choice.

Educational sociologists now are studying how different populations' everyday experiences in and out of school foster recurrent patterns of educational attainment. This book asks *how* an individual's ascribed and achieved statuses influence her or his attainment. For some time now, researchers have shifted their attention to the growing realization that *where* a person attends college is critically important to understanding the links between social class and educational attainment, persistence, and occupational achievement (Useem and Karabel 1986). Differentials in access to particular kinds of institutions are an important aspect of how the educational system contributes to intergenerational transmission of status, since high-status students are both more likely to attend college and more likely to attend a good college than are low-status students (Karabel and Astin 1975).

While an individual's academic achievement is clearly a key determinant of college attendance, the interplay of a student's social class background and the high school's organizational contexts and processes appear central to the question of *where* an individual attends college. And, since most students get into their first-choice college, the key issue addressed in this book is how a student's social-class background and the high school's social and organizational contexts shape a senior's choices about higher education.

Theoretical Framework

Why does the higher education opportunity structure work differently for different students? This study builds on Weberian theories of status groups and intergenerational status transmission, as well as on organizational theories of decision making to highlight the importance of diversity of organizational context and status culture background on individual decision making. Status group theories shed light on the differences in attainment rates of various socioeconomic status groups, while organizational theories provide insight into how and why a school context can influence individual behavior.

Three propositions guide this study:

1. a student's *cultural capital* will affect the level and quality of college education that student intends to acquire;
2. a student's choice of college will make sense in the context of that student's friends, family, and outlook, or *habitus*; and
3. through a process of *bounded rationality*, students will limit the number of alternatives actually considered.

Cultural capital (Bourdieu 1977) is that property that middle and upper class families transmit to their offspring which substitutes for or supplements the transmission of economic capital as a means of maintaining class status and privilege across generations (Bourdieu 1977a). In other words, middle and upper class families highly value a college education and advanced degrees as a means of ensuring continuing economic security, in addition to whatever money or financial assets can be passed along to their offspring.

The cultural capital theoretical framework of Pierre Bourdieu has been important in many of the new sociological studies that focus on how and why class status plays a role in educational achievement. For this research I am situating high school students' college-choice processes in their social, cultural, and organizational contexts and am demonstrating the essential role of values, as they are embedded in everyday life, in decisions about where to go to college.

Status groups are social collectives that generate or appropriate distinctive cultural traits and styles as a means to monopolize scarce social and economic resources (Weber 1978). Elite status groups have appropriated educational credentials for the intergenerational transmission of social status and power (Bernstein 1977). Cultural capital is a symbolic good that is most useful when it is converted into economic capital. Although all classes have their own forms of cultural capital, the most socially and economically valued forms are those possessed by the middle and upper classes.

Cultural capital is precisely the knowledge that elites value yet schools do not teach. With the complexity of the types of college choices in mind, this study treats a college education as a status resource or symbolic good in our society. Cultural capital is of no intrinsic value. Its utility comes in using, manipulating, and investing it for socially valued and difficult-to-secure purposes and resources.

Bourdieu observes that those with high cultural capital have clear strategies of how much and what kind of schooling each generation should have. A student's disposition toward school is important because to maximize or conserve cultural capital one must be willing to consent to the investments in time, effort, and money that higher education requires. Parents transmit cultural capital by informing offspring about the value and process for securing a college education, and its potential for conversion in the occupational attainment contest.

DiMaggio (1982) found that cultural capital not only mediates the relationship between family background and school outcomes, but it also may have its greatest impact on educational attainment through affecting the quality of college attended. He also suggests that cultural capital possibly may play different roles in the mobility strategies of different classes and genders.

Bourdieu also uses the concept of habitus to refer to a deeply internalized, permanent system of outlooks, experiences, and beliefs about the social world that an individual gets from his or her immediate environment. According to Bourdieu (1977b), habitus is a common set of subjective perceptions held by all members of the same group or class that shapes an individual's expectations, attitudes, and aspirations. Those aspirations are both subjective assessments of the chances for mobility and objective probabilities. They are not rational analyses, but rather are the ways that children from different classes make sensible or reasonable choices for their own aspirations (Macleod 1987). They do so by looking at the people who surround them and observing what is considered good or appropriate across a variety of dimensions. To elaborate on Bourdieu's work, through proposing the concept of entitlement, students believe that they are entitled to a particular kind of collegiate education based on their family's habitus or class status.

This study will also extend theoretical notions of habitus and present evidence that it exists not only in families and communities but in organizational contexts. Showing how organizational habitus exerts an influence on individual decisionmaking, I investigate the variety of organizational contexts and status cultures in high schools as they have an impact on seniors' college choices. This is not an assessment of an individual counselor's effectiveness, but rather an analytic description and assessment of the impact of the broader school climate on the creation of an organizational habitus that limits the universe of possible college choices into a smaller range of manageable considerations. I am looking at the school as the mediator of collective social class consciousness in regards to the processes and outcomes of college choice.

Bounded rationality refers to behavior that is rational but limited by the cognitive constraints on decision making. High school seniors cannot and do not consider all of the 3,000 possible collegiate choices (Simon 1957). Most people settle for satisfactory alternatives due to time and resource limitations. The alternatives people consider are influenced by their physical location, social networks, and environmental stimuli, as well as the anticipated goals and consequences for college.

Students face a complex decision when choosing a college. According to March and Simon (1958), individuals perceive their choices by scanning the environment around them, which often is limited by geography and their usual social contacts. The high school senior's frame of reference and perceptions are conditioned by the evoking mechanism—the high school context for college choice. Through this research I will demonstrate how this context can have a differential impact on students from different class backgrounds and I will use bounded rationality to frame the analyses of school habitus.

Just as Bourdieu's individual-level perspective includes objective probabilities and subjective assessments, an elaboration of the college-choice process as it takes place in high schools must account for both the cognitive and affective processes underlying the premises for decision making (March and Simon 1958). Individual student behavior will be influenced by the flow and content of information and the school's explicit expectations that highlight or downplay specific options (Perrow 1979). These information flows and expectations are, in turn, based on assumptions about how familiar students are with basic information, prerequisites, and specialized college choice vocabularies.

The high school is an intermediate institution in the educational system. Student continuation to college is voluntary, and in contrast to the elementary-secondary link, this transition is driven by individual achievement and motivation. The interinstitutional linkages between most high schools and colleges are, at best, loosely coupled (Weick 1976) and, at worst, there are no links whatsoever. Colleges are fairly autonomous and have individualized admissions rules despite some similarities of procedures and generalized norms. Some high school counselors help individuals manage and overcome loose coupling. A few schools (private preparatory, some Catholic, and some public schools) have tight coupling, which includes ample college preparatory and advanced placement classes, institutional networks between the high school and specific colleges, and well-developed flows of information about the college admissions process.

In the late twentieth century, some upper-middle-class students view college as a major personal investment needing extensive, careful planning. The application process is increasingly pressurized and speeded up, guidebooks are omnipresent, seniors are preoccupied with choice, and some parents now start strategic planning for college in their child's elementary or preschool years. Many new phenomena from the public and private sectors influence the college choice process: independent counselors (McDonough 1994 and 1997); consortia which arrange for high school counselors to visit college campuses to become familiar with and recommend those campuses; self-help and SAT coaching guidebooks and software; statewide clearinghouses on college placement; and magazines devoted to extolling the benefits of private education, which are marketed to students stratified by SAT test scores and socioeconomic status.

Colleges and universities increasingly compete with each other for students, and admissions is more than just the composition of a student body, it is survival. Admissions policies reflect economic, political, and academic considerations. As competition increases, individuals and institutions resort to mimicing successful behavior to deal with uncertainty and to ensure success (DiMaggio and Powell 1983). Skyrocketing competition for students has led to a rise in marketing by moderately selective institutions in response to enrollment declines predicted for the mid-1970s, and only now materializing in the 1990s. Fearing life-threatening enrollment declines, colleges have dramatically increased marketing budgets and spend $1,700 on average to bring in each new student. All of the best marketing techniques have been brought to bear on college admissions: marketing and public relations consultants, focus groups for prospective students, institutional repositioning, and enrollment management (Schurenberg 1989). Along with this unrestrained media blitz, colleges make substantial efforts for providing educational equity and increased access to higher education by ethnically diverse students groups.

The heightened competition in college enrollments has left many students feeling uncertain about their ability to compete effectively, which has changed students' application practices as well as led to the rise in independent educational consultants and the SAT industry. The use of SAT coaching services for college application enhancement also has risen: revenues for Stanley Kaplan—one of the largest SAT preparation services—doubled between 1983 and 1988 (*Time* 1988). Various media feed this uncertainty with articles appearing regularly in national magazines like *Time*, *Newsweek*, and *Money;* local newspapers across the United States; professional journals; and college alumni magazines, including all of the elite colleges.

The institutional structure of the college admissions environment creates and legitimates certain social actors—in this case, college applicants—and makes cultural rules appear normative and universal, thus eliminating alternatives (Meyer et al. 1987). Within the organizational sector of college admissions, the actions of applicants represent more of an enactment of predetermined scripts than of internally directed, autonomous choice complete with motivation and purpose. College admissions environments shape the organizational structure and culture of high schools as they relate to college guidance. The low-SES students and schools in this study do not participate in these scripted college choice behaviors, but instead are shaped by a local opportunity structure and limited financial resources. Both of the high SES schools of this study are, however, shaped by a national, volatile, competitive college admissions environment that is further influenced by a local community culture focused on prestige.

Significance of the Study

This book illuminates the ways in which school context shapes student tastes for particular types of postsecondary institutions. I analyze class-based differences in family values and how they affect the way in which students organize their college-choice processes and how students think about the range of "acceptable" institutions. The empirical evidence in this book documents how these class-based differences in aspirations in turn affect the stratification of opportunity structures at the higher education level and beyond.

I identify status culture and organizational environment patterns. For example, working-class students see academic achievement as set, an inflexible fact of their admissions potential. For upper-middle class students, achievements are seen as somewhat manipulable through SAT coaching classes, the use of private counselors, and their presentation of self.

Students' feelings about their college years as a time for breaking away from family, neighborhood, and friends combine with their perceptions of geographical constraints to delimit the area over which they cast their college choice net. All students seem constrained by the need to be able to get home quickly in an emergency or as a fix to bouts of loneliness, although families' economic resources mean rich and poor students view those distance constraints differently. Furthermore, the values of community and loyalty held by working class students are quite different from those of the upper-middle class students, who view their community more as a geographically unbounded social class than a neighborhood.

Cost considerations of college vary greatly between rich and poor students. The role of "safeties"—schools that students apply to and are sure they can get into—varies for students from different social classes. The economically advantaged students are looking for good liberal arts schools and are desperate for safeties, but only safeties that will have prestige and will satisfy their status-conscious fellow students, parents, and neighbors. Finally, most students also are looking for colleges from the context of their current habitus: colleges that match the same supportive environment in which they have been nurtured during high school, colleges that are consistent with their own personal values or personalities, or colleges that provide a needed contrast to the high school experience.

This book offers new and important questions for further research: When is the organizational context salient? At what points and for what types of students can the organization influence individual decision making? And, finally, what has changed or what is stable in the college admissions environment?

Organization of the Book

Chapter Two introduces all of the college-bound seniors through vignettes of how they made college choice decisions. I write about who the students are and where they actually ended up attending college and include profiles of their high school grades, SAT scores, and college choice processes. This introduction of each student focuses on two major elements: the range of how they went about deciding which colleges to consider and theoretical issues to be dealt with later.

Chapter Three provides a detailed introduction to each of the school's environments, offering information on when counseling begins, the counselor caseload and orientation to the college-choice process, and the school climate in general. Chapter Four is a cross-case analysis of the role of counselors and support services at each school and their impact on shaping the aspirations of that school's college-bound students, with a limited analysis, where relevant, of the impact of curriculum and teachers. I present evidence for organizational habitus as both a theoretical construct and a practical reality.

Chapter Five asks and answers the question How did family, friends, finances, and high school jobs influence how students arrived at their respective colleges? I provide insight into parents' precollege educational investment choices, notably the choice of a private high school and the use of a private counselor. I examine the role of social capital—family and friends—in shaping aspirations for "right" college choices. Chapter Five also focuses on excerpts from parents and students on how they view the college admissions process and on insights into the emotional and practical difficulties inherent in the college choice process. I also provide an analytic summary and integrative analyses of the role of the school with analyses of the role of family and friends.

Chapter Six summarizes how students' aspirations develop and vary across socioeconomic groups and school contexts, showing how structural and social processes influence college choice decision making. I summarize the evidence for how class-based differences in aspirations affect the stratification of opportunity structures at the higher education level and beyond.

Research Methodology

This book presents rich case studies of individual college choice processes and the organizational contexts that shapes those choices, as well as a cross-case analysis of the high schools. It also situates high school students' college choices in their social, organizational, and cultural contexts and demonstrates the essential use of values as they are embedded in a habitus of decisions about where to go to college. Because I only want to vary social class and the organization of guidance in these high schools, I am holding gender and race constant and only interviewed white females, the largest population of higher education enrollees in the United States today.

To arrive at issues of bounded rationality and school influences, I chose students from schools that had weak or strong guidance support systems, defined by counselor-to-student ratios, as were schools that had a majority high or low SES student population. Because this was a study of a student's cultural capital as it influenced her college choice decision making, SES was instrumentally and contextually defined for this study as a two-part, crude dichotomous variable. A student was classified as high SES if both parents had bachelor's degrees and were employed in professional occupations, while low SES was defined as both parents not having bachelor's degrees and not being professionally employed. The school was considered high SES if over two-thirds of the students were from high SES families, and low SES if over two-thirds of the students were from low SES families. Within each school I selected students who matched the SES of the school and one who did not, to see if these students were able to access the school's resources differently because of their own or their family's knowledge of college.

The students were drawn from four California high schools, which were a mix not only of high and low social class status contexts, but also high and low college guidance operations (Table 1.1). I defined a strong guidance operation by counselor-to-student ratios and looked for schools that fit the average student-to-counselor ratios across the four types of schools (see Chapter Four): a low SES and low guidance school (public), a low SES and high guidance (Catholic) school, a high SES and low guidance school (public), and a high SES and high guidance (private preparatory) school.

I explored the concept of habitus by interviewing a parent, best friend, and school advisor for each target student, and attempted to untangle the kind and amount of influence each of these people had on the students. Accordingly, some best friends came from a wider range of GPAs, ethnic groups, and parental educational and occupational backgrounds.

I conducted in-depth interviews with twelve white females who were middle-range academic performers (GPA range 2.7–3.4, SAT range 700–1250), specifically three college-bound seniors from each of four high schools ($N = 12$). I also interviewed those students' best friends ($N=12$), parents ($N=12$), and coun-

TABLE 1.1
Guidance Support/Socioeconomic Status

	Lo/Lo	Lo/Hi	Hi/Lo	Hi/Hi	Total
Seniors	3	3	3	3	12
Best Friends	3	3	3	3	12
Parents	3	3	3	3	12
Counselors	1	1	1	1	4
Total	10	10	10	10	40

selors ($N = 4$). Each interview ranged from one to three hours and was preceded and succeeded by several phone conversations.

Since this study's main intent is to understand the interaction of social class and the high school organizational context, I reluctantly controlled for ability, race, and gender. The model can later be tested for males, other racial and ethnic categories, and higher- and lower-ability students. I chose to focus on middle-range academic performers because in many ways the choices of the lowest-achieving students are constrained to community college options, until they can remediate their high school experiences; and the highest-achieving students follow more predictable patterns of applying to the most prestigious public and private schools that are available to them.

I collected transcript data on all students. I also administered questionnaires to the rest of the students in academic-track classrooms in each school to gather data on a broader group of the students' peers about: college plans, parental educations and occupations, first thoughts of college, when and how often standardized tests were taken, how many colleges students knew about, and how many applications were filed.

In my interviews with the college counselor at each school I collected information on the postsecondary destinations of all of the students at these schools, as well as information about the schools' total resources devoted to college preparation. I asked counselors about how college guidance was organized, the assumptions of the college assistance program, and what kind of course advisement was provided to college-bound students.

Interviews with counselors included asking questions about students' aspirations and their potential for college. I collected observational and written data from bulletin boards, college counseling centers, computer data sources, and other school, curricular, and guidance materials. All of this was used to assess the available resources for guidance and information on the background characteristics of the school's students.

I interviewed guidance counselors at each school and collected the names of three students who fit the study's criteria and those students who might be willing to be interviewed. Each counselor selected the study's subjects from a list of students who met the GPA and parental qualifications criteria. Table 1.2 shows the students, best friends, GPAs, and colleges.

TABLE 1.2
Interview Subjects, GPAs, and Colleges

	Paloma School	*Gate of Heaven High School*	*University High School*	*Mission Cerrito High School*
Target Student	Judy (3.2) DePauw	Karla (3.2) UC-Berkeley	Constance (2.9) CSU-Long Beach	Lucy (2.7) West Valley C.C.
Best Friend	Kimberley (3.2) So. Methodist	Laura (3.1) U Bologna	Cindy (3.4) CSU-Long Beach	Julie (3.0) West Valley C.C.
Target Student	Leah (3.2) Middlebury	Cathy (2.9) San Francisco State	Margaret (3.3) Mills College	Samantha (2.8) DeAnza Comm. C.
Best Friend	Sarani (3.0) U Oregon	Darla (3.3) San Francisco State	Marilyn (2.6) U Montana	Edie (4.3) UCLA
Target Student	Susan (3.2) Pomona College	Charlene (2.9) San Francisco State	Sara (3.2) Boston Univ.	Carol (2.7) San Diego State
Best Friend	Candy (3.3) UCLA	Jackie (3.5) San Francisco State	Rebecca (3.6) Brown Univ.	Kay (2.8) West Valley C.C.

*All names are pseudonyms.

After each phone call and interview, I wrote annotated field notes detailing overall environmental and contextual impressions. These included interview summaries, which noted the presence or absence of examples of conceptual categories or anything else particularly noteworthy about the interview. Periodically I wrote analytic memos which I used to explore issues related to developing understandings of the conceptual categories derived from the framework.

Interviews were conducted in a rolling sample format. I analyzed the collected data using the constant, comparative method: I analyzed each interview and specified, modified, affirmed, or rejected conceptual categories in an effort to build theoretical insights from the grounded data observations (Glaser and Strauss 1967). I refined the codes throughout data collection and analysis through the continuous comparisons of incidents, situations, categories, and typologies across students and schools.

Limitations

In searching for a California average of guidance counselors-to-students, a State Department of Education demographics researcher revealed that it was not available. Although the State Department of Education collects a lot of statistical information, there was no demand for counselor-to-student ratio information. The best available estimate was that there were 5,229 full-time equivalent guidance counselors in the state and 4,488,398 students for a ratio of 1 counselor for 858 high school students. Guidance counselors were among the first educational positions to be cut after Proposition 13. This high ratio and lack of statewide data collection attention indicates the low level of priority given to guidance services and the potential policy significance of the need for understanding the role of school guidance for college planning. However dramatic California's counseling ratios are, nationally, the average counselor-to-student ratio is 1:323, which suggests that there is little individualized attention given to students by school counselors in any state.

On a more practical level, aside from the college preparatory school counselor, most counselors were not very familiar with their students or their families. The Catholic school counselor, after working with her students over their entire high school career, said: "It's hard for me to remember the kids, because I just see them in mass amounts for 20-minute periods." Even students who felt that they had a good rapport and visited their counselor often experienced that visit quite differently than the counselor. A student at the public high SES high school spoke of visiting with the counselors "three times a week" and thought she had a good relationship with her counselor; however, his impression of her visits was that he had "relatively little" contact with her.

With such a small sample, this study is meant to be both theoretical and exploratory. It has attempted to go beyond the quantitative studies' emphases on the what and how many kinds of questions, and instead focuses on why and how students make decisions about where to go to college. I chose a qualitative methodology to provide insight into the motivations and behaviors of students as they go through the college choice process and to find out why students make the choices they do. By understanding the meaning of students' choice processes, educators and policy makers can devise meaningful and effective policies to address culturally equal opportunity. Given the restrictions of race, gender, and the number and types of high schools, the findings of this study cannot be generalized to wider populations. However, the information and findings of this study can be used to design further research on influences in the college choice process.

Finally, there is a certain amount of randomness within each individual's consideration of colleges and, possibly, in the final choice. However, the specific choices are not as important as the process that the students go through and the set of outcomes they define as acceptable. The school, family, and community all influence college-bound seniors and shape their aspirations and sense of entitlement. Social class affects the resources that individuals have at their disposal to make choices about where to go to college. This study will show how high school seniors today make decisions about where to go to college and why that is an important issue of educational equity.

CHAPTER TWO

So Many Ways to Choose a College

What follows is a description of how twelve typical high school graduates and their twelve best friends chose their colleges. These students' best friends, parents, and guidance counselors also are an important part of this story because they highlight factors that influenced how these students, and others like them, chose their colleges. The families of these girls and the high schools they attended influenced how these girls went through the process of choosing a college, what schools they considered appropriate, and where they ultimately ended up attending college.

The ultimate choice of college is important because, despite the gains in enrollment in advanced education beyond high school, there still exist differentials based on class and race in participation in higher education. Moreover, there are noticeable differences in attendence at colleges and universities with differing rates of prestige, graduation, and occupational success.

The image of college attendance portrayed by this meritocratic society assumes a natural fit between talent and ability in the pursuit of a collegiate education. I challenge that assumption and look at how other cultural factors mediate talent and ability. I explore how patterns of choosing colleges are a result of the confluence of school, family, community, and class cultures. Further, I suggest that there is currently a new institutionalized admissions environment that is helping to rationalize and define the appropriate ways of selecting the "right college" for students of different social class backgrounds and academic preparation.

Paloma Young Women

Five subjects in this study are graduates of Paloma School in northern Silicon Valley in California, while an additional best friend of one of the Paloma young women is from a public, middle-class high school. Paloma is a private, all-girls school in a quiet residential neighborhood in a community where the average

19

home sells for well over half a million dollars. The campus resembles a rambling home and grounds more than it does a school. The average Paloma student files four college applications. In these students' graduating class, there were fifty-six graduates, 100 percent of whom went on to college, 96 percent specifically to four-year colleges, and 42 percent to out-of-state schools, with one-third of all Paloma girls going on to some of the nation's finest schools.

This college preparatory school was founded in the early 1900s, specifically to prepare girls for a nearby prestigious university. There are a little over 325 students in the seventh through twelfth grades, the vast majority American white or foreign students, and many being students of color. Class size averages thirteen students, and the curriculum is varied, with many advanced classes. The five Paloma girls in the study were A–/B+ students at this college preparatory school and attended Middlebury, Pomona College, UCLA, Southern Methodist University, and DePauw.

Middlebury is one of the bright stars in the higher education firmament. It is a highly selective (28 percent admit rate), prestigious, liberal arts college in the Northeast. It enjoys a favorable rating as a perennially "hot" college among high school seniors. Middlebury students graduate at a rate of about 70 percent, and many of its alumni attend graduate and professional schools. Other alumni make their mark in many professional careers and enjoy comfortable middle- and upper middle-class lives.

Leah Stein wanted to enjoy the fall foliage and the crocuses' heralding of spring on the Middlebury campus. While a Paloma senior, Leah, with a 3.22 GPA and 1250 SAT scores, applied to four highly competitive, private, liberal arts colleges and two of the University of California campuses, Berkeley and San Diego. She originally was waitlisted at Middlebury and decided she would attend Colby over UC Berkeley, her top alternate choices. When word came that she was being offered a place in the Middlebury freshman class of 1993, Leah jumped at the chance to attend her dream school.

Leah had focused on attending a prestigious college as far back as the seventh grade. At that point, she decided she wanted to attend Paloma to help reach her college goal, after hearing about the school from a middle-school teacher. Her parents, both psychologists, shared her aspirations and were supportive of her efforts in every step. When Leah began the process of narrowing her college choices, she spent a lot of time with Paloma's college counselor, Mrs. Ball. Leah and Mrs. Ball consulted regularly as Leah sought to figure out what was important to her in a college environment. After much reflection on her experiences at Paloma, Leah decided that a small, intellectually nurturing setting was most important, thus she carefully researched private colleges. As most Paloma students do, and as they were encouraged to do by Mrs. Ball, Leah applied to the UC schools as backups.

Leah's best friend, Sarani Zagreb, is an engaging artist, slightly but charmingly offbeat. Sarani, who did not attend Paloma, went to the local public high school in the community where she and Leah grew up together. That community is deeper in the heart of Silicon Valley than Paloma and is a comfortable upper-middle class neighborhood where most parents are college-educated and employed in professional careers.

Sarani is an only child, the daughter of a successful engineer who encouraged her to expand her horizons and find the right school for her, saying he would find the money to finance her choice, whatever it might be. In fact, in telling her not to apply for financial aid, he said: "Don't worry about money. You can go wherever. We'll worry about that when you get accepted, you don't have to do it before.... don't worry, we can afford it." Believing her choices were limited only by her ability to be accepted, Sarani's college selection process was centered on finding a school with exceptional art training, with a strong preference for attending college in the Northeast, where she had spent a summer at Phillips Academy at Andover, attending art classes.

Sarani forged her own way in sorting through the considerations of what kind of college would be best for her, not availing herself very much of her high school's guidance services. Aside from being clear in her vision of wanting a strong art school, she consulted only with her parents. Her mother supported her explorations, whatever they were, and her father had a strong desire for her to receive a solid liberal arts training. Sarani's dream school was the Rhode Island School of Design. Her neck-in-neck second and third choices, Boston University and the University of Massachusetts at Amherst (U Mass), were concessions to her father's liberal arts concerns. She ended up in the Pacific Northwest at the University of Oregon, which was her fourth choice. This turn of events came about when acceptances came in and choices had to be made. Her father, at this point, made a final assessment of the monies available and determined that a state school was the only feasible alternative. U Mass accepts very few out-of-state students and Sarani was not one of the lucky few.

Sarani was heartbroken, not because she had no interest in the University of Oregon, but because she felt betrayed. After having done the work of researching schools, filing applications, attaching emotionally to her select few and tensely waiting for those precious acceptances, she felt bitterly disappointed that she could not accept the offers of the schools she allowed herself to dream about:

> I spent hours and hours writing the essays, picking them up, picking apart, writing letters, filling out my applications perfect[ly], making xerox copies, giving them the money . . . you don't get it back. And then finally, when I got accepted, it was like 'Whoa . . . you can't go. It's too expensive.'

Judy Taylor worked very hard in the competitive Paloma environment and struggled to keep up with her academically talented classmates. Her GPA was identical to Leah's, although her SAT scores were 250 points lower. She approached her college choice process with a mixture of hope and realism:

I think that everybody starts out with the same ten schools, with the Ivy's and all that. I know I did. And then once you see what your GPA is and your scores, you become more realistic as time goes on. . . . new schools come into the picture after you realize . . . what you have to deal with.

Judy's process for making choices about her range of acceptable colleges involved extensive help and emotional strength from her mother, consultations with her high school and her private college counselor, and using the highly rationalized criteria of looking only at private, liberal arts schools with strong Spanish language curricula and semester abroad programs. Geography also played a big, rather specific, role in her planning: to be considered seriously the college had to be out of California, a reasonable plane ride home, and located relatively close to the airport. The unusual level of travel specification was a result of Judy's family owning a travel agency and being very cued in to travel amentities, especially to how easily and quickly Judy could come home if and when she wanted to.

Eventually Judy defined a list of acceptable choices: three UC schools and six small colleges in the Midwest, South, and Northeast. According to Judy, the UC schools were under consideration by her parents because of the attractive cost, yet according to Judy's mother, Judy applied to the UC schools to see if she could get accepted. The private schools were Dennison University, DePauw University, Southern Methodist University, Trinity College, Boston College, and Middlebury College, the latter being a very long shot. Judy was concerned about finding the right atmosphere at her new school and looked for a college that had a lot of the strengths of Paloma: small, nurturing, and personalized. DePauw won out:

I like that kind of atmosphere . . . like Paloma. . . . A lot of attention, extra help, professors teach the classes . . . I just like the attention . . . really strong tradition . . . the permanence of tradition. . . . It allows people to . . . really become close.

Of the colleges where Judy was accepted, the UC schools were never serious choices, SMU seemed "too materialistic and big," Trinity was geographically too remote (the college was several hours away from the airport) and the people "were not like me." When she visited DePauw, as she had visited all of her college choices, she fell in love with the people, the atmosphere, and the attention. Although she had been waitlisted at Boston College, which previously had been her first choice, she happily set her sights on DePauw. Suddenly, the grueling process was over and all was right in Judy's world.

Kimberley Scott, Judy's best friend, happily attended Southern Methodist University, the school where one of her older sisters is an upperclasswoman. Kimberley's college choice process is a story of strong family influence, early admissions action, and a protracted illness during the senior admissions season. Like her best friend, Kimberley used both her high school and a private college counselor to help define her range of choices. Kimberley's mother, her two older sisters, and, to a lesser extent, her father, were the major players in Kimberley's selection of a choice set and in making final decisions.

Kimberley described her mother as "active in our lives and she was thinking all the time where . . . could I go to school." In fact, Kimberley's mother had been thinking actively about Kimberley's college choices since she was about fourteen or fifteen, when Kimberley's oldest sister started on her college choice process. What solidified Kimberley's choice was that in the fall of her senior year she decided to apply for early action at SMU. Soon after getting her early action application in to SMU, Kimberley contracted mononucleosis and was absent from school for about eight weeks. Because of these unique constraints, Kimberley was not back in school until early December, was trying to catch up with her school work, and was not able to complete and mail any of her intended applications, except to the three University of California schools.

> I was still really weak and really behind, and so I just said well, I'm into SMU and I know that's where I want to go . . . what's the point of running myself into the ground and filling out all these. . . . it was a January 15th deadline for UC and . . . just in case I didn't want to go or in case I changed my mind.

The other schools she would have applied to were the University of North Carolina, Duke, Georgetown, William and Mary, Emory, and Boston College. The reasons she articulated for her choices were that she wanted any UC school or a school "back East," near a major metropolitan area, a needed contrast to Paloma and one that had a good liberal education program. The latter consideration stemmed from her intention to become a doctor and Kimberley felt that a good, general, undergraduate curriculum would prepare and position her well for medical school.

On this topic she consulted with her father, an eminent cardiologist and medical school professor who advised her on choices to consider for both undergraduate and graduate schools. William and Mary was on her list of intended applications because her private counselor insisted that she apply. Kimberley's mother raised many college choice considerations, for instance, suggesting Kimberley go back East in order to use college as a time for geographical experimentation. Yet, because of repeated knee surgeries, Kimberley was not interested in the colder Northeast, thus only considered schools in the South and Southeast.

Finally, Kimberley and her sisters had been really close growing up. All three went to Paloma and shared a certain understanding and camaraderie. She said, "I've missed that since they've been gone." So she decided she really wanted to go to school where one of her sisters was in attendance, either Duke or SMU. She was clear that she only wanted to go where one of her sisters felt very positive about her school. Her oldest sister was happy, but not always or overly so, at Duke. "I think she likes it. She doesn't love it, she doesn't have a passion for it, like my other sister has a passion for her school."

Like Judy, Kimberley's sister's unhappiness partially stemmed from geographical constraints: because of the time involved and airline connections to get from Duke to California, her sister could not easily fly home for a weekend. Meanwhile, her other sister at SMU was ecstatic about the people, the weather, and being near a big city, all of which also was important to Kimberley: "She just loves it, she loves the people. Mostly it was her . . . in fact it was all of her influence that made me decide to go there." Thus Kimberley's choice seemed easy and comfortable.

For Susan Harriman, getting into Pomona College was the culmination of a lot of careful research, soul-searching, and buckling down to hard academic achievement. Although going to college had always been a given, it was not until her junior year that Susan realized the need to dramatically change her attitude toward achieving academically, especially by improving her grades. Partially, Susan was aware that she needed to get serious about her grades and about college preparation, but just as significant was when, in eleventh grade, her advanced placement teacher took her aside and urged her to "kick yourself into shape and work even harder. . . . You could get into some really great schools."

This teacher "was a big believer in" small, private, East Coast colleges, and discussed them with Susan. The idea was appealing to Susan because she had never attended a large or a public school. In fact, Paloma was the biggest school she had ever attended. Later, Susan broadened this group to include some private schools in Southern California. She also knew that a small school was important so she could get to know the teachers. Susan knew her learning habits well enough to see this was a prerequisite for engaging with her studies.

Because Susan had a lot of friends who were seniors when she was a junior, she panicked when she saw them get into schools and still not know where they wanted to go. She thought: "Hey, there's got to be some rational, logical way to go about this." So, Susan began her college choice process in a highly organized fashion. She papered her bedroom wall with a chart. Across the top of the chart were names of schools she and her teacher had identified; down the side were the ten characteristics of a college environment that were important to her, including: small (3,000 to 5,000 students), liberal arts, private, quality faculty and low student-faculty ratios, location, Division II women's soccer team, and a campus that had school spirit, was intellectually intense, and politically active, and finally, (although a consideration she found difficult to assess) "a place where women were valued as much as men."

She went through the colleges' viewbooks, filled in data, and then put gold stars on the schools that met her needs. After a proliferation of gold stars, she realized the limits of this kind of rationality and was keenly aware of the vagaries of matching student to college.

You have to visit the school and you have to just sort of like it or not. The decision is really irrational when it finally comes down to it.... a small, liberal arts school looks a lot like the next small, liberal arts school on paper.

Having identified her decision criteria, Susan applied to fourteen schools, including four "safety" UC schools—Berkeley, UCLA, Santa Barbara, and San Diego. The other (private) schools were: Oberlin, Barnard, Occidental, Claremont McKenna, Middlebury, Tufts, Franklin and Marshall, University of Southern California, Vassar, and Pomona.

She is very happy with her choice—Pomona is small, where professors know and care about students and not just about research projects. There is a lot of political activism on campus, including feminist and anti-rape groups. Moreover, Susan really felt that at Pomona women were valued as equals. She found and developed her intellect at Paloma and set as a high priority that her collegiate academic experiences should challenge her to hone her abilities to think critically.

Candy Whitcomb did not attend Princeton, her dream school. Instead, she attended UCLA, "not a school I pictured myself at" and a striking contrast in size and atmosphere to both Paloma and Princeton. A bright and ambitious young woman, Candy's college choice process offers an interesting glance into playing by all of the new rules, maximizing all of the chances, yet nonetheless being disappointed and ultimately ending up in a distant choice college.

This whole thing is just insane. I think I'm the classic case of buying into this college thing and everything that goes along with it, and everything they told you not to do.

Candy was a senior at Paloma a year before her best friend, Susan, and availed herself of all of Paloma's college counseling expertise, as well as signing up to work with a private counselor. This counselor coached her for the SATs, which she had Candy take three different times. Although she tried to help Candy by suggesting thematic directions and attempting to edit application essays, Candy refused her help. Academically, Candy was a strong student at Paloma, had SATs averaging 1170, took advanced placement tests for History and English, and had high achievement scores for English, Math-1, and Biology. Candy also was involved in a number of extracurricular clubs and sports.

As a junior she twice visited East Coast colleges. During her senior year, Candy applied to four UC schools—Berkeley, UCLA, Santa Cruz, and San Diego. She also applied to Vassar, Middlebury, Columbia, Princeton, Brown, Trinity, Georgetown, and Colorado College. She was rejected at Columbia, Brown, and Georgetown and accepted at Trinity, Colorado, Vassar, and Middlebury, all of the UC schools, and "I got waitlisted at Princeton. That's when the whole awful mess started."

Candy's plans began to go haywire when she started to think about her options for the next year and began to factor in money considerations. "So at the end of my senior year I—financially we weren't sure if we could swing one of the private ones, which were all around 20 [thousand dollars]." Her mother's employee benefits offered approximately $7,000 in tuition benefits, which she could apply to the cost of a private college for Candy. However, given eligibility requirements, which were tied to the length of Mrs. Whitcomb's employment, the tuition reimbursement would only be available beginning in Candy's second year. Because of this financial consideration, Candy "just sort of decided that I was going to take the year off."

As she elaborated, the decision about taking a year off had as much if not more to do with the Princeton waitlisting:

> I really had wanted to go to Princeton and they waitlisted me . . . "you were accepted and you just happen to fall on the wait list . . . you're the standard that we need." . . . So I sort of bought into that and thought if I take this year off and call them up and say 'I really want to go to your school and you waitlisted me,' there would be no reason for them not to accept me.

After deciding not to defer any of her acceptances because she did not want to jeopardize her chances of getting into Princeton from the waitlist, particularly thinking long and hard about Middlebury, Candy waited to hear from Princeton the entire summer after her graduation. In August, when she heard the freshman class was full, she then pursued her year off. Through family and friends she lined up a year-long job at the Office of Management and Budget in Washington, D. C. As an eighteen-year-old ordinary employee, Washington was not what Candy had expected. It was not as much fun as freshman year of college, or as pressureless as doing something with a deferred admission year, or even as valuable a learning experience as a structured internship program with other people her age.

So, in Spring 1989, Candy began the agonizing process of applying to colleges and waiting for admissions' decisions for a second time. She applied to Princeton, Harvard, Yale, Barnard, Stanford, and the same four UC schools. Unfortunately, this time she was not as successful: Princeton, Harvard, Stanford, and Yale said no; Barnard and all of the UCs said yes.

This time, however, money played a considerably more important role in making the final decision. Her parents were not as interested in paying similar amounts of money for Barnard as they would have been for Princeton:

> There's this sort of feeling, I think, for my parents and also for me that it's worth it to do this at Princeton, but is it worth it to do for Barnard? . . . Again it's sort of twisted, but there you go.

Thus, Candy found herself at UCLA, a school of 33,000 students, after spending high school in the small, intellectually, and personally nurturing environment of Paloma. Candy is a human postscript to this study of seniors and their college selection process, because she has gone through the process twice and, as she summarizes it, not only ended up with "even less desirable choices" the second time around, but more importantly, has come out feeling victimized by the process, with a damaged sense of self.

The Women of Gate of Heaven High School

Located in the heart of a major American city, Gate of Heaven High School is the academic staging area for the second five of this study's subjects. Again one best friend attended a surburban, public high school. This all-girls Catholic high school has existed since 1821 and is run by a small, progressive order of nuns. Although autonomous, it is under the broader jurisdiction of the superintendent of Catholic schools for this city.

Gate of Heaven is located a few blocks away from a major university in a quiet, mostly residential and lower middle–class neighborhood of the city. However, the 450 Gate of Heaven students are drawn from all over the city and a few come from nearby communities. A little over half of the students are white, and a little less than one-third are Asian and Pacific Islander. Hispanics and Black students each make up 7 percent, while 3 percent are Native American. The senior class had 117 members, and class size averages around thirty pupils. Students from Gate of Heaven, on average, submit two applications to colleges. All but a few continue their education within the state of California. The curriculum is focused on college preparation: 91 percent attend college directly after graduation.

For the students from Gate of Heaven High School who are considering which colleges to attend, cost is a substantial factor, while ability is a modest limitation. Although these students have the same A–/B+ grade point averages as the Paloma students, their SAT scores average substantially less. Geography plays a significant role in students' college choices, as it does with Paloma students, but the meaning of geography is constrained by money and perception of distance. Four of the five Gate of Heaven students in this study attended San Francisco State, and one attended UC Berkeley. The best friend attended the University of Bologna in Italy.

Cathy Ross had a 2.9 GPA at Gate of Heaven High School. She worked for the Dean of Students to offset some of her tuition costs but was not involved in any extracurricular activities at her school. Cathy's parents, a big city policeman and a civil service secretary, were generally supportive of her going to college but not especially knowledgeable about what she should be thinking about or planning for in terms of college. They never asked her about what she might like to major in or where she should go. Cathy herself was ambivalent about college and about why it was important to go. She has witnessed up close in her own family that college does not always pay off, therefore it can be a risky proposition. Her brother, who was enrolled in the local community college when Cathy was a senior, already had a job in which he was paid more than Cathy's uncle, who has a graduate business degree. Cathy also saw this incident as proof of the role of luck in her opportunity structure perceptions.

Cathy was somewhat tired of going to school and primarily thought of a college education as career insurance. She wanted to major in business because she saw this as a potentially lucrative career possibility and because it took fewer years of schooling than her original choice, which was to be a lawyer. Cathy was more (but not overly) focused on someday being a mother and raising a family, rather than on having a career. She saw having an education and career as a safety net in case she got divorced or, as in the case of her own mother's motivations, as being useful for securing the "luxuries" a family in the 1990s needs, like a parochial school education for the children and a second car.

Cathy only applied to Sacramento State and San Francisco State because she was afraid of being away from home and missing her friends. Also, she was wary of her own maturity and motivation and wanted to live at home so her parents could provide her with the discipline she feared she lacks. Moreover, she had a very good after-school job in a law firm that she wanted to keep, thus Cathy decided staying in her home city meant she could attend college and still keep her job. Cathy did not want to "live off" her parents for college, and although they told her not to worry about money for college she did not want to be a burden to them. In Cathy's mind, there was a clear relationship between the cost of college and where one chooses to enroll. She said that if she anticipated paying for college herself, she would see no reason to pay for San Francisco State when San Francisco City College is much cheaper.

In Cathy's college schema, UC was out of the question. Although her grades and SATs would put UCs way out of her reach, Cathy's claim was that UCs were not a possibility because minorities have special admissions preferences and financial aid policies that favor them.

Darla Lopata was Cathy's best friend, even though, aside from their shared religion class, Darla was in different classes at Gate of Heaven. Her family also was supportive but not knowledgeable about colleges, especially her father, a mailman who collected college catalogs and guides for her from people on his route. No one in her family had gone to college, except a cousin who spent two years at the UC Santa Cruz and dropped out because she was still undeclared about her major and uncertain of her educational and career plans.

Darla's Gate of Heaven counselor tried to encourage her to apply to UC schools, but Darla thought she would feel more comfortable on a California State University campus. She was especially intimidated by the academic competition it took to get in and to remain at a UC, even though she had a 3.3 GPA in high school. This counselor also fought with Darla to take advanced placement English, even though Darla wanted to take accounting and other courses in which her friends were enrolled. Darla looked only at large state colleges with business curricula, an interest partially spurred by her part-time job at a real estate office. She did not regard community colleges very highly because she said going to one would "be like nothing." Most of her friends went to community colleges or were unsure about going to college at all. Darla wanted to be at a school where she had friends, because she did not want to be alone.

Money seems at times to have played a large role in Darla's college choice process. Her parents were paying for college and she wanted to pick one that was "reasonable." She only looked at state schools because of tuition costs and did not seriously consider going away to school because of the expense. Even the highly subsidized University of California campuses seemed too high-priced. However, college was cheaper than her high school tuition and money for basic attendance was not seen as a problem by Darla or her parents. So college as an educational experience was not out of Darla's range of financial possibilities, but college as life experience—living away from home—was.

Charlene Hauptman had a 2.9 GPA. Like many of her Gate of Heaven counterparts, her parents were supportive but not knowledgeable of the college choice process that their daughter was going through. Charlene's mother does not have a college degree, although for some years she has taken art classes at the local community college. Charlene's brother, who is ten years older than Charlene and went to San Francisco State, talked with her extensively about going to college and specifically about attending his alma mater. Charlene's mother and brother were key in her choice to attend San Francisco State, but in very different ways.

Beginning with Charlene's seventh and eighth grade teachers, they have been influential in introducing college and suggesting solid academic preparation. Moreover, her junior high school counselor advocated for Gate of Heaven High School and later, for Catholic colleges as well as introduced Charlene to notions of better and worse schools. Gate of Heaven High School also was quite influential in shaping Charlene's college choice process, because the guidance program, facilities, and staff were supportive and helpful. Charlene's counselor assisted with application details and strategies. Charlene was the only Gate of Heaven student in this study to actually visit colleges. Even though Gate of Heaven was able to introduce wider geographical horizons to Charlene, her geographical vision was still limited—she only seriously considered schools that were very close.

Charlene considered colleges where someone she knew had attended and would recommend them. In spite of this, friends' choices were not very influential. "I figure college is so big you're not . . . going to see your friends anyway." The college's proximity to Charlene's home (in spite of having visited far-away schools) was an extremely important consideration. Charlene had a major interest in accounting and had a good after-school job that influenced her college choice. Having a job with a decent future was something both Charlene and her family viewed as an important consideration when picking a college.

For Charlene, money was a major influence. Finances for going away seemed prohibitive and private schools seemed unreachable. Her parents had "offered to help," but putting the choice and financial package together was Charlene's responsibility. Charlene's mother and brother expressed their strong opinions that the local state university was good enough for her brother, therefore should be good enough for her. From their perspective, Charlene did not need to consider anything else. She did not apply for financial aid because she had an inheritance from her grandmother for her college (and high school) tuition and she did not think she would be eligible, since tuition at State is low and she would be living at home.

Although Jacqueline Davis went directly on to San Francisco State after graduating from Gate of Heaven, she had a difficult time putting her life back together after she spent an extended period of time fighting to stay alive and recovering from serious brain injuries, after being struck by a car as she walked through an intersection of the city. While at Gate of Heaven, Jackie had high hopes of attending college. Her father, a waiter, had graduated from San Francisco State with a bachelor's and a master's degree, as had her mother. Her stepmother also graduated from San Francisco State with a bachelor's degree. Jackie Davis's family was very influential in helping her cultivate a "taste" for education for its own sake, especially for a broad liberal arts education. "Pretty much" her whole family had gone to four-year colleges, except her stepbrother and stepsister, who were ambivalently attending San Francisco City College while Jackie was a Gate of Heaven senior. Although her father, mother, and stepmother were all college-educated, none were professionally employed.

Even though Jackie had a 3.5 GPA, she only applied to San Francisco State and did not consider any other college. She filed her college application early because, by doing so, she believed she had a better chance of getting in. She had thought about studying nursing, but was not in any way prepared academically. She had not taken the proper high school science classes nor had she applied to the nursing program at SFSU, opting instead for general admission. Although most of Jackie's friends were going to SF City and San Francisco State, this was not a major influence. Financial aid also was not a consideration for Jackie. She only considered living at home and going to school locally, so the cost of college seemed reasonable to her. Her family was paying for school, with the bulk of the financial support coming from Jackie's grandmother, who paid for the Gate of Heaven's tuition.

Karla Franco, torn between extremes—Italian versus U. S. universities, public versus private colleges—struggled with where she should go to college. The middle child of an Army medical doctor father and an Italian-educated teacher and translator mother, Karla benefited some from her older sister's college experiences while working through her own college choice difficulties. Karla applied to three UCs and San Francisco State as a backup and considered the University of

Bologna because she grew up in Italy and wanted to return. Berkeley was her first choice because it was nearby yet far enough away, and she could room with her sister.

Both of Karla's parents were well-educated and concerned about Karla going to a "good" school, but they vehemently disagreed about what schools were good and where she should go. Karla tried to stay out of the fray. For financial reasons, Karla's father would not allow her to consider a private school, yet her mother wanted her to consider Stanford University or Santa Clara University because she thought they were better schools.

Karla was highly involved in extracurricular activities at Gate of Heaven. The school had a significant influence on Karla's college choice process, especially in helping Karla stay on top of information and deadlines. Moreover, Karla's teachers and counselor were helpful in passing along opinions that San Francisco City College was not a good choice for Karla.[1] She was the only Gate of Heaven student in this study to take the SAT achievements, and she took the Math, English, and French tests. Her English class prepped her for the SAT vocabulary section.

Most of her school friends applied only to SF City or San Francisco State, except for one friend who applied to a UC but was rejected. Her best friend is going to the University of Bologna, which Karla seriously considered but decided against. Karla's boyfriend was a positive influence and probably the main reason she applied to UC Davis. She talked of managing her conversations with school friends about college choices because she feared rejection and she did not want to "rub it in" that she was applying to UCs and they were not.

Laura Frescotti, Karla's best friend, went to Gate of Heaven for one year and then transferred to a suburban public high school. Laura was only interested in attending college in Italy, where she is a citizen and had spent most of her life. Laura's father is a Italian consulate official. Laura did not do much about her college choice process in her senior year of high school because she planned to move to Italy in the summer after her senior year and then apply for admission to the University of Bologna, where she would live with her father's family. Money was not a consideration, nor was staying in the United States for college.

University High School's Women

The next six college-bound seniors are graduates of University High School (UHS) in northern Silicon Valley, a public school that is about a two-minute walk

---

1. Karla's father considered it a backup to UC Berkeley, since SF City College had an arrangement whereby admission to UC Berkeley was guaranteed after completing two years at SFCC.

from Paloma. Both are situated in a community where the average family income was over $61,000 in 1989, nearly twice the national average. The UHS campus is sprawling, safe, and typical of an upper middle-class public high school in California. The average UHS student files nine college applications, with the range being from three to five. There were 365 graduates, 89 percent of whom went on to college. This college preparatory public school had 1,280 students in the ninth through twelfth grades. The curriculum is tracked, with great differentiation in college preparatory classes. The six UHS girls were A–/B+ students and attended Boston University, Brown University, Mills College, University of Montana, California Polytechnical University at San Luis Obispo, and California State University at Long Beach.

Sara Ornstein is a well-adjusted, cheerful student with a 3.22 GPA. Sara has an older sister who was attending UCLA while Sara was a senior. Sara's mother owns and operates a travel agency, while her father is a Silicon Valley engineer. Sara's parents started a Hebrew day school in New York, where the family used to live, and passed along to Sara a real dedication to the value of education. Sara is very connected to her parents, and they have been active and welcome participants in her college choice process. When asked who has been most influential in the college choice process she said: "Parents, just the three of us. Long before anybody ever asked any question."

Sara had a well-managed, carefully constrained college choice process. She seriously considered and applied to seven schools, one of which, Brandeis, she felt was unrealistic but which had always been her dream school. Sara had a deep-seated urge to attend college on the East Coast, even though her parents wanted her to stay closer to home in California. She applied to Boston University, Quinnipiac, Brandeis, Cornell, Simmons, University of the Pacific, and University of Southern California.

Sara received assistance from a private college counselor who recommended six schools to which Sara should apply.

> I researched them and I wrote letters to them and asked them to mail
> me stuff. And I did everything that I had to do . . . And then I de-
> cided which ones I wanted to apply to and I did it.

Sara also was able to be more restrained in her college choice considerations because she felt she had clear directions for her major and career: she wanted to be either a physical therapist or a doctor, thus she looked for colleges that offered physical therapy programs. Sara and her family were focused on the fact that she was an average college-bound student with a test-taking problem: "My SATs are not up there at all. They're very low, because I cannot take any sort of a standardized test. . . . my grade point average is okay, but it's not superior or anything." Together they worked with SAT coaching classes and her counselor to package Sara's application portfolio, putting the best case forward.

Sara's limited (six) college application process was mostly positive for her, although she felt at odds with UHS norms.

> It's the least number of anyone who I know ... very bizarre feeling. ...
> all these people are applying to so many schools because they don't
> know what they're going to get into, and then here me with six
> schools, and only two of them I'd really seriously consider, possibly a
> third.

Sara's friends were all academically superior students, which she viewed as a plus because that way she was not in direct competition with them. They shared her interest in attending an East Coast school and are now attending institutions like Brown, Cornell, and Princeton.

Sara's best friend, Rebecca Feinbaum, ended up at Brown University and was the student in this study who applied to the largest number of schools, fifteen. Rebecca had three file drawers with information on each college she considered. She had an extremely rationalized process and started to become more "realistic" after taking the SATs and a subsequent SAT preparation course.

> You start looking through the ... college guides and ... think about
> well, what is the probability that I could get into this kind of a school.
> Does this kind of school fit my personality or not. Whereas before you
> just think oh, Princeton has a pretty viewbook ... I've always heard of
> Princeton, I always thought I'd go to Princeton, whereas it may not be
> a realistic choice. It may not be something that is attractive even to you.

College was always a taken-for-granted reality for Rebecca because "when you're little, you think you'll go to Harvard or something really prestigious like that. ... I ... and everybody else always assumed that I'd go to college." Rebecca's college choice process was fraught with anxiety over the arduous steps of applying, waiting, and facing possible rejection, further complicated by not always feeling supported by her friends. Often, these students were in competition for the same limited number of college spots. "In the beginning, I felt like such a jerk because I didn't want anybody to apply to certain places that I was applying."

Rebecca, however, developed a philosophical approach to rejections and managed the negative emotions of the college choice process quite well: "When you get rejected ... you have to look at it that. ... It's ... not a good match for you. ... that's a really healthy way of approaching rejections." In spite of this philosophy, Rebecca also had "anxiety attacks" on occasion. For Rebecca, looking for the "right" college was a task that involved matching the atmosphere of the college with her personality. Rebecca says she always asked college admissions officers, "What's the community like? ... Are the students happy?"

Rebecca's mother was a key player in her daughter's college choice process. This strong mother-daughter relationship was quite positive for Rebecca, and even though there were rebellious and tense elements of this parent-child relationship "she was supportive and nagging." Rebecca's mother was especially adamant about hiring a private college counselor and consulting with friends and relatives who were knowledgeable about college admissions. Rebecca knew she was quite advantaged in her college choice process by having college-educated parents and friends who offered tidbits of information, as well as the money to apply widely and retain the services of counselors or coaches when necessary. She also was very aware of her privilege in not having cost considerations play much of a role in her college choices.

Margaret Avalon attended Mills College, although choosing to attend a women's college was not always easy. Margaret's mother has a college degree and her father dropped out of a Ph.D. program just before completing his dissertation at UCLA. He is now an engineer for the city in which they live. Margaret's dad was influential in bringing her back onto the academic track when she strayed in ninth grade and also was influential in Margaret's developing academic interest in anthropology. Margaret was very comfortable with her college choice process and settled into her place in the academic hierarchy of UHS: she graduated from high school with a 3.33 GPA. Margaret took "normal" math and sciences courses, yet also took one honors English, and AP English and German in her senior year. She sees academic ability as manipulable yet historical and expresses regrets about her slow academic progress in her early high school years. In addition to the SATs, Margaret took the English, math, and history achievement tests. For financial reasons, she did not take an SAT prep course, as did most of her peers.

Although she is the fourth of four children, Margaret's siblings offered little role model assistance about how to choose the right college environment. Margaret's siblings include an older brother who did not go to college and two older sisters, one who was a senior at a design school and another who, by default, was attending community college. Margaret's college choice process focused on Mills College, Cal Poly, the University of Oregon, and UC Santa Cruz, UC Davis, and UC Riverside. She considered Oregon because of its location, yet was discouraged by out-of-state tuition costs. Her interest in journalism lead her to seriously consider Cal Poly.

Money was an issue from the moment Margaret began thinking where she should go to college. She might have considered more private colleges but was greatly influenced by money and geography because California state scholarship grants for private schools are applicable only if the student goes to school within California. Margaret had a sophisticated knowledge of the state financial aid system and money availability because of her older sister's financial aid experience. "I need to stay in California for monetary reasons if I'm going to go to a private school. There's absolutely no way without any money from the state for me to go to a private school out of state."

Mills College entered Margaret's field of college vision when her mother suggested it. Margaret visited Mills College for one day of classes and an overnight stay in a dormitory. She knew what she wanted in a college environment: a pleasant living, yet intense learning, environment. Because of her interest in Mills College, Margaret also faced a lot of pressure from her peers and some adults about women's colleges. Just by considering a women's college, she had to fight stereotypes and some derision. This led her to advocate for women's colleges in general and to feel a part of Mills College while still at UHS.

Her junior high school prepared her for the high academic expectation environments of both her high school and college. In high school she took classes at the local junior college. UHS has a detailed college choice process, beginning with curricula planning in the ninth grade.

> It was good guidance to bring a kid in there and ask them. I think most kids say 'Yes, I want to go to college.' And they know that a 9th grader isn't thinking about it . . . they set it [curriculum planning] up, and then if you have problems with it, you can come back in and fix it.

UHS habitus is for many applications, some of them unnecessary applications—they were just safeties. "I have applied to very few schools compared to the people at my school. . . . if you want to go to a school on the East Coast, you've just got to apply to twelve . . . that's what they feel like." Margaret found UHS to have intense peer pressure. She explains this by talking about CSU Chico: "People [are] saying, 'Well, that's not a good school.' . . . that's peer pressure. What if two years ago I wanted to go to Chico State? I might really feel threatened by the people that tell me it's just a bad school."

Marilyn Clayton was not really focused on external things, especially school, grades (2.66 GPA), or careers. She was inner-motivated and introspective. Her parents did not place a lot of pressure on her but both they and she always assumed she would go to college. "It's one of those things where in junior high you think, 'I'm going to high school and college.' You just kind of assume it, especially around here in this kind of community." She is now attending the University of Montana. Money was not an issue at all in Marilyn's college choice process.

Marilyn's father took charge of everything in her life, including her college choice process. His organization was helpful but annoying, often leaving Marilyn with a sense of incompetence. She applied to one school, her father's alma mater. According to her, her dad was overly involved in her college choice process: first, without her knowledge or permission he signed her up for a summer program at the University of Montana in her junior summer, then he completely filled out her college application, leaving her only to sign it. Yet because of that summer program, Marilyn knew people at UM before arriving. Another consideration in choosing UM was that she loved the area and had relatives nearby.

Marilyn was very interested in pursuing art and her long-term interests in commercial art or graphic design drove her to look for a residential, all-encompassing college experience. Yet she realized she wanted more out of college than she could get just at an art school "I began to think I'd kind of like the American college life. . . . I didn't want to miss out on anything." This focus coincided nicely with the University of Montana, even though the art department there struck her as being "unimpressive" after she received information about its offerings.

She felt high school was pressure-filled, beginning with the policy of forcing freshman to develop a four-year plan for college. College was seen as the only viable path after high school and, according to Marilyn, "most people just applied to, depending on how much they can afford, they applied to state or UC schools." Marilyn was keenly aware that applying to just one school was at odds with the average UHS senior's behavior. She felt the students and teachers were too grade-obsessed, and teachers sometimes made inappropriate jokes or made a public, humilitating spectacle of reading grades aloud. Her disaffection with school influenced the way she viewed course requirements. Subsequently, she met them haphazardly.

Marilyn found it difficult at UHS to be marginal or different in college choices, especially as the college waiting game heated up while students were tensely waiting to hear about their acceptance status.

> Everyone's under all this stress right now because most people haven't been accepted anywhere, and it was quite a while ago when I got accepted . . . they want to know my situation, and I say I'm going to University of Montana. And they either like try to restrain from laughing . . . or they say "Why!?" . . . That bothers me.

She expressed frustration over having to explicate her motives for an anomalous college choice to her peers. Just as many of her peers self-consciously admitted, Marilyn knew that if she did not like her college choice she could transfer, that it was not an immutable decision. Yet something in the UHS habitus made students who were aware of this fact approach the college choice process as if their lives would be over if they did not get into a prestigious college.

Constance Evans had a 2.94 at UHS yet did not know about the PSATs until her counselor told her about them. She had not thought about where to go to college until junior year, when her friends started talking about it. Constance's parents were supportive but neither attempted nor succeeded at weilding any influence. Her father acknowledged that she completed the whole college choice process herself and "came to us with questions. We didn't have the immediate answers for all of it. It was a puzzle."

Constance was positively affected by the UHS four-year plan and, luckily, her high school's graduation requirements matched entrance requirements for most four-year colleges. She completely relied on information received from her school, because she herself was not at all sure of college entrance requirements. Constance frequently visited the Career Center. "I've checked out books on the schools, I've checked out videos. I've gone in and talked to Mrs. Dean, who's the college advisor." She gives the school major credit for getting her through the process and realizes that the school's information was not enough without her own aggressiveness. "You have to go in there and keep asking questions." UHS was even more helpful in giving "insider tips" to Constance, such as advising early submission of CSU transcripts before CSU requested them.

Constance felt that the normative expectation at UHS was for private, selective schools "mostly in California," as well as UCs and CSUs. UC Riverside had a specific reputation for being the easiest of all the UCs to get into and was heavily applied to by UHS students. Constance was not at all interested in UC, which was definitely against the UHS grain. She saw other students making their college choices for the wrong reasons: places where they knew lots of people or where there were party schools. For Constance, the "right" reasons were for the education and intended majors.

Constance was a poignant case of a first-generation, college-bound senior. Although she ended up at CSU at Long Beach, she lacked college habitus and found out what she needed to know on her own a bit haphazardly. She faltered in trying to describe why she thought it was important to visit schools before applying. She talked about wanting to be comfortable, and moreover, she did not know which schools were public or private. "I learned a lot by just going down and looking at the colleges. I mean there are tons of things I didn't know about."

Constance applied only to state colleges—San Diego State University and CSU-Long Beach, Cal Poly, and Johnson and Wales in Rhode Island. The latter choice was interesting in that Connie discovered this school as a result of their pursuit of her after a PSAT student search. This school waived the application fee, thereby making it impossible for Constance to resist: "What the heck, I might as well apply and see if I could get in." Most UHS and Paloma peers would never apply in such a way. Some of her college choice direction was based on a vague career interest in business, yet Constance lacked confidence in her abilities. She believed that knowing what you wanted to major in was an essential part of college decision making "I thought it would be easier . . . if I decided something I could focus on, what I might want to study, it might be easier to look at colleges [otherwise] that school may not be good in what you want to major in."

Constance made visits to two of her schools before applying and felt that this was an absolutely essential step for her "I didn't know anything about the school, and about the area . . . I don't think it's a good idea to apply to a college that you haven't visited . . . I think it's important to feel comfortable where I'm going." Yet she did not visit Cal Poly because she talked to people she knew who went there and viewed a video. She never considered visiting Johnson and Wales, seemingly suggesting that it never was a serious choice. In fact, Constance's school visits were due to her best friend, Cindy Lane's initiative.

Constance felt UHS's habitus was too stressful. "I don't want to take on all that stress. I don't think it's necessary . . . I just don't want it to like totally ruin my life if I'm not accepted to a certain college." Constance felt a bit overwhelmed by the process and the pressure.

There's so much you have to do that it gets kind of complicated and you feel like you're just being . . . overwhelmed by stuff. It's real . . . nagging. I guess once the whole process is over, it's okay.

When asked how she will pay for college Constance said, "I don't know," while her father said, "Good question." She knew she needed to enlist the aid of her parents and take the initiative herself about figuring out how to finance college. Constance also knew when and how to use her counselor, although she was not exactly sure how extensively UHS could help her with financial aid. Her lack of prior information or college habitus hampered her somewhat. "I'm not ever exactly sure . . . where that financial aid is coming from. I just know . . . those are the forms I need to fill out." Constance and her stepmother were concerned about how many loans Constance might be expected to incur, about being a blended family, about general equity issues related to financial aid, and about the wealth of the area in which they lived and if that was factored into financial aid equations. Her stepmother also was concerned about the expectations of Constance working to support herself, yet facing job shortages in a small college town, and concerned about Constance being overloaded with work and school.

Cindy Lane graduated with a 3.38 from UHS and attended CSU at Long Beach. Both of Cindy's parents went to San Jose State University. Although her dad loved his alma mater and wanted his daughter to go there, he understood her need to get away from home. Cindy's dad and stepmother were supportive but did not initiate helping her. "They're really open about it, and once you get them started on it they don't want to stop. But I can't recall a time where my dad'll bring it up himself. If I bring it up we can talk for hours." They will, however, pay for her college.

Cindy wondered if her parents "realize that there is more pressure now than there was when they started. I think that maybe they feel that there's just as much, but maybe not more." Cindy applied to CSU Long Beach and San Diego State, two of the same colleges to which her best friend Constance applied. Her criteria for narrowing down her choices was to look for schools with her intended major, Recreation and Leisure Studies. She eliminated CSU at Northridge because of its location, yet included San Diego State "just because it's a really pretty campus."

The PSATs acted as a trigger for Cindy to begin thinking about her college choice process. She met with her counselor to discuss schools that she could get into given her scores. The counselor told her that the only UC she could "get into right now with your grades is Irvine." Cindy felt a little unprepared. "All these names of colleges just came flying at me, and I didn't know one from the other. And it's like I still don't really."

The Women of Mission Cerrito High School

The last six subjects of this study are graduates of Mission Cerrito High School, a suburban public high school in northern Silicon Valley. MCHS is located in a

working class residential neighborhood in a community where the average home
sells for about $250,000 in California's inflated real estate market. The campus is
relatively large, yet nondescript. The average MCHS student files three college applications. There were 400 seniors, 70 percent of whom went on to college, 15
percent specifically to four-year colleges and 55 percent to community colleges.
Only 2 to 3 percent of MCHS students attend out-of-state colleges. MCHS has a
majority of white students, with small numbers of Hispanic and Asian students.
This town founded its first public high school in 1863. There are a little over 1,800
students in the ninth through twelfth grades. The curriculum is varied, with many
students taking vocational classes. The six MCHS girls in this study were A–/B+
students in high school and attended UCLA, San Diego State University, West Valley Community College, and DeAnza Community College.

Carol Lincoln was a quiet girl and knew few people who had gone to college. Her older brother not only was unsuccessful and dissatisfied with school, but
in Carol's senior year he still was in a continuation high school. Carol's parents had
briefly attended a local junior college and had generalized expectations about
Carol going to college, but provided little actual help. Carol's counselor was
equally uninvolved in her college choice process, thus Carol was left pretty much
to her own devices. After being ignored by the counselor, she forged ahead on
her own and began to review the few college information books and individual
school catalogs available at her high school. After she generated a list of a few possible schools, Carol again consulted her counselor, whose only comment was that
two of her choices were quite pretty and adjacent to the beach.

Not only was her high school not very helpful, in fact many of her problems in preparing for college began with poor junior high school counseling. This
affected her admissions eligibility because she did not take many of the classes she
needed for CSU and UC admission. Carol was accepted at her first-choice school,
San Diego State University, on the condition that she make up her deficient
course preparations. With her 2.74 GPA and a 970 SAT score, Carol also applied
to Texas A & M, San Diego State University, and CSU at Long Beach. The only
school in which she was offered a placement was San Diego State, which of course
she accepted. Interestingly enough, Carol decided to apply there on the "spur of
the moment," something her counterparts at Paloma and UHS would never do.

Carol, who was uncertain about what she might like to study or pursue as
a career, was not focused on types of curricula available as she thought about
where to go to college, although geography certainly played a role in influencing
the colleges Carol considered. Leaving home was an important factor to Carol.
She visited Texas A & M while on a trip to see her aunt and claimed no other attributable trigger for being interested in that school. Because of that visit to Texas
A & M and because of a small circle of friends that were bound for four-year colleges, Carol began to consider and only applied to those schools. Most of Carol's
friends were going to Chico State or the local community college. Carol herself
thought of the local junior college as a backup. She thought little about how to

pay for college, except that she filled out the financial aid forms and anticipated that it would work out.

Carol's best friend was Kay Baptiste. Her divorced parents briefly attended junior college, as did her older brother who attended and then quit after six months. Kay's mother is a teacher's aide and her father is an iron worker. Her parents were supportive of Kay's plans to attend college. Kay looks up to her father a great deal and often seeks him out for advice. In spite of this, Kay's parents were not at all knowledgeable about colleges or how to apply. She did not know a lot of people who had gone to college; most of the people she or her parents know are court reporters and teacher's aides. However, some of her parents' friends were modestly influential in making minor suggestions about her college choice process, although most suggestions related to terminal community college credentials.

Kay was wary of the higher education opportunity structure, much like Cathy Ross from the Catholic school. She had a real awareness of the pitfalls of going to community college, the number one danger being that many who attend never graduate or go on to four-year schools. Besides Carol Lincoln, few of Kay's friends were going to college. Of those who were, most did not talk with her about their college plans. Kay did not feel she got much, and certainly not enough, information from her friends about how she should make choices about college.

Kay was uncomfortable about Carol Lincoln going away to school. She was concerned about Carol's leaving and the impact that that would have on their friendship, as well as the fact that they were taking very different life paths. For Kay, this raised questions about whether or not it was right to go away and questions about the impact of leaving on those who were left behind. Kay cannot imagine herself going away to college. She thought that when it came time to transfer from her community college, she would attend San Jose State. Paying for college was a consideration in the broadest of possible terms, but was not much of an issue since Kay was going to attend the local community college. Her father had some money saved and his boss would contribute some money, so she was not really worried about financing for school until she goes to what she calls "a real college."

Samantha Shaeffer's family has always entered higher education through a junior college. However, Samantha had always imagined that she was going to go to a four-year school because she "always thought that I was better than a JC. I thought JCs were frumpy and I didn't want to go to one." Prior to deciding on a junior college, she had decided to shoot for a CSU and not a UC "because State required less. . . . Less expensive. . . . Easier to get into." Her dyslexic father barely got through high school, yet he believed that a college education was a prerequisite for success. His considers himself lucky to have a good paying job and Samantha believed that his opportunities were "not going to happen for us, and so you got to go to college."

Samantha's mother informed her that since she was not a star student (GPA 2.8) and therefore would not be eligible for scholarships, she should attend a community college. She attended the local community college and lived at home, with her parents paying for her college education. Her mother constrained Samantha to the local community college because of financial considerations and because Samantha did not know what she wanted in terms of a major, career, or life in general. This was a significant theme for Samantha and many of her contemporaries at MCHS. Their parents felt that as long as their children were uncertain about what they wanted to do for a major or career, then living at home and growing up a bit more was appropriate before going away to a four-year school.

Samantha found the switch to a community college difficult and had to emotionally readjust to her new prospects. Although she decided to attend DeAnza, one of the premier community colleges in the state, she had to deal with the negative image of community colleges.

> A lot of people go to JCs first . . . they're getting pretty much the same education without paying so much, and then they get a better idea of what they want to do. It's not so frumpy anymore, since I'm doing it.

Samantha's friends went to very different places: "I hang around with some real smart girls and they're . . . all going to a four-year, except maybe one or two." She had a close-up view of their situations and pressures, although watching them was "depressing because I wanted to go so much, but . . . I'll get there." It caused some internal conflict to have her friends going to places she would like to be able to consider. Samantha had separate groups of friends:

> There're some that I have classes with, a lot of classes with, because they're just like normal level, and those are the ones going to State. All the other ones have AP classes or advanced classes. I'm not in those.

Samantha never talked to any of the teachers or counselors at her school and felt she was poorly advised. Her list of lapses in the counseling process was extensive: her counselor did not know she was college-bound; she was scheduled into a sophomore biology class that did not meet the CSU requirements; and MCHS' counseling occurred only when the counselor came into a class and talked about general requirements. "They just talked to everybody in the whole class at once. It wasn't like individual." Beyond these complaints, much of MCHS advising happened through written guidelines, and Samantha often found that problems were identified too late.

Edie Tashimi, Samantha's best friend, was one of MCHS' academic superstars. Valedictorian, with a 4.3 GPA, and a 1220 SAT score, Edie did very well in her achievement exams in English, History, French, and Civics. She was on student council for four years and was "in everything." Edie's mother and father both have bachelor's degrees. Her mother is an elementary school teacher and her father is a computer programmer. Her older brother was attending UCLA in her senior year of high school. Edie's college choice process was very rational: she looked for colleges with good medical programs that she could later apply to, and since she was interested in minoring in art, she looked for schools with good art programs. Money was not a part of Edie's college choice decision making. She is attending UCLA, although Stanford University was her first choice. Because of the weather and the distance, Edie did not think about going to college out of California. She applied and was accepted to UC San Diego and UC Riverside, but felt that UC San Diego was a little too far away and Riverside was her third choice. She investigated UCLA while visiting her brother there. Also, at UCLA she knew other people and had friends in the area, which she considered a plus if she ran "into a problem."

Edie's only influences in selecting her college were "parents, friends, and just the colleges themselves." Edie believed in visiting colleges to check them out for how they felt and felt it was important to know people attending these places, thereby making them more accessible. She did benefit somewhat from her brother's process. "I just kind of picked up on the basics." Edie's parents were incredibly supportive and knowledgeable but insisted that Edie make her own choice. They recommended "UCs in general," specifically noting campuses about which they had heard positive comments. A lot of her parents' information came from their friends, whose children were attending various schools.

Edie has a stratified friendship structure: some of her friends have ambitions similar to her own, while others were going to junior colleges. She behaves differently with these two sets of friends.

> With my school friends, we don't really talk about college too much,
> because a lot of them are just going to go to community colleges and
> they're not really going to go out to college. But with my other
> friends that go to different schools, we talk about it, about what it's
> going to be like.

Lucy Baker's parents are both college-educated. Her father is a sales manager for a computer firm and her mother is pursuing a master's degree in counseling, while interning as a school counselor. Lucy's parents will pay for college. As with most of her friends, Lucy attended a junior college, even though she was accepted at San Jose State and Chico State. She originally intended to go to a CSU school but then began to have doubts about following through on her acceptances because she felt uncertain about why she was going to college and what she should study.

Starting at the junior college level seemed like the right thing to do, according to her father and friends. Lucy thought about going away but was unsure. She wanted a small school, one close to home. She considered Chico State and

San Jose State University because at each of those schools she knew people and felt she would not be totally alone. Also, she considered Chico State because it was only three and one-half hours away from home and because she had a friend who attended the school. She saw this friend as being very much like herself, and Lucy figured if this woman could move away and succeed, so could she. She talked very little with her friends about college.

Lucy did not worry much about college acceptances. "Most people get in if you have those requirements and stuff." However, based on conversations with college friends and teachers, her expectations of college were that a four-year college was more than she had been prepared for at MCHS, and she doubted her ability to write papers for college since she did not have to do that at MCHS. Lucy was keenly aware that some students at her school were prepped for college and that the tracked nature of schools was set early on. Lucy's college choice process sneaked up on her. When it came time to begin her college choice process, Lucy went to her parents and said, "Help me, I don't know what to do." They said they did not know what she wanted to do and asked "what I wanted in a college, did I want to go somewhere big or small, or far away or up close." She also talked to her counselor, then, with her parents, looked at the MCHS booklet for colleges "I could get into." Lucy used the MCHS booklet that was distributed to seniors and "tells a little bit about all the colleges." The senior counselor had workshops about filling out applications and "he's brought in speakers from the junior colleges." Moreover, he had a parents'-meeting. The senior counselor also visited classrooms to "give you sort of what you need to get into a college, a four-year, or junior college, or university."

For Julie Carlson it has always been "when you go to college . . . it's never been do you want to go to college." She lived with her mother who is a kindergarten teacher with a degree from a CSU school. Her father is a CSU-educated engineer, with a degree in business from UC Santa Cruz. "I always had the images from my mom and my dad . . . college is the best time of your life . . . you meet your lifelong friends there." Her father was extremely involved in her education and pays her for good grades. "Education is just the most important thing . . . my grades are like . . . a job to him." Julie's dream schools were interesting when compared to the dream schools of UHS and Paloma students: "Naturally you want to go to, oh, let's go apply at UCLA, San Diego State, and Chico State." Geography also played a role in Julie's college choice process: in addition to staying in state, her parents wanted her to live within driving distance. This set her boundaries at Sacramento State in the north and Cal Poly in the south. Julie only considered the California State Universities because UCs seemed too pressured-filled. "The state university would be enough of a load to handle, because I don't think I can really do well or feel good at a university."

Julie considered her parents and friends equally influential in her college choice process. She applied to San Francisco State, Sacramento State, San Jose

State, and Sonoma State. Like her best friend Lucy, Julie did not have a clue about her career plans and speculated that maybe she should be a homemaker. She did, however, think a lot about deciding where to go. Her mother wanted her to live at school, but Julie's dad felt that if she could not make up her mind then the best thing would be to go to the local junior college until she was ready. Julie was concerned that although the junior colleges in the area were good, junior colleges in general do not have a good reputation.

> West Valley's nickname is Waste Valley. . . . I consider it as a first step, but some people are embarrassed to say, 'Well, I go to community college.' I'm not embarrassed to say that. A lot of people go there, and I think if it's the best thing for me, then that's where I've got to go.

Julie felt strongly that most MCHS students were not going to go to a four-year school and that they should fight the community college stereotype. "They're all going to end up in a junior, so we better wake up and realize that that's where they're going."

Julie, like Lucy, was not very confident about her MCHS college preparation. She looked for a college where she would have good teachers and receive personal attention, not one where "they don't care if you're there or not . . . and the classes are so big. I like one-on-one attention and not just being a number." This was the original reason her mother encouraged her to apply to Sonoma State. Her MCHS counselor advised her to go to the community college and then transfer. This advice was influential in lowering her expectations, in spite of her mother's encouragement to aim for CSUs. Julie first received this advice in a class, although it was later repeated in an individual counseling session. The general advice to her entire class had as much influence as the counselor's one-on-one advice:

> Mr. Sirotti said that was probably the best thing. Not just me, but for anybody in general in my class. . . . He asked me where I applied and told him, and he said, "Well, that's fine but that a really good way to do it is to go to a two-year and transfer to a four-year.

Almost all of Julie's friends were going to junior colleges, although she and her friends were comfortable with the college choice of one friend, who was aiming higher. Julie's parents assumed all responsibility for financing college, for which Julie was grateful.

CHAPTER THREE

Four High Schools, Four Social Worlds

Paloma School

Discretely tucked away in a quiet, affluent suburb less than two-tenths of a mile from (the public) University High School is Paloma, an independent girls school. The entrance to both secondary schools is off of the same busy suburban street. So obscure is Paloma's presence that the local police often set up a speed trap across from the administration building to catch the drivers who quickly cruise this wide avenue, ignoring the "Slow School" sign.

The brown-shingled administration building resembles a grand home and is in keeping with the turn-of-the century architecture of the neighborhood. Adjoining it are several, tasteful institutional-style buildings, which stylistically blend in with nearby homes. Covering one city block, the grounds include a dormitory, chapel, fine arts center, and ample classrooms, laboratories, and an impressive library. The athletic facilities include indoor basketball and volleyball courts, three tennis courts, and an Olympic-size swimming pool. In the center of the campus, live oaks, palms, and redwood trees circle a grassy playing field, which sports field hockey nets.

Paloma is a college preparatory boarding and day school for girls whose central goal, since 1907, has been "to graduate young women who are eager to learn and act responsibly in the adult world . . . to maintain the highest standards in all areas—academic, social, moral." The thirty-six faculty members hold a total of twenty-four graduate degrees from an impressive array of private, prestigious colleges and a few state universities from the United States and abroad.

There were fifty-six members of the senior Paloma class and 316 students in grades seven through twelve. Paloma had forty resident students. Paloma students were predominantly from California, although there was a scattering of students from other states and around the world. The students were relatively homogeneous; they were white and came from affluent families. What ethnic diversity there was came from a small population of Asian and Asian American students, a tiny population of African American or Hispanic students, and foreign nationals. Although the college counselor felt that "culturally, it is so rich to be teaching in this school"[1] because a small percentage of students come from all over the world, she was aware that Paloma still had progress to make in diversifying their American population. "We very much would like to increase the number of Hispanic and black students. We've got a good number of Asian kids, but we really do need an increase in Hispanic and black kids."

Tuition is over $7,000 and about 20 percent of the student body was awarded financial aid on the basis of their ability and need. Most parents held college and post-baccalaureate degrees, while many of the remaining parents had some college education.

Paloma students from the senior class preceding the students of this study collected a stunning number of college acceptances and modeled attendance at some of the finest public and private postsecondary institutions. The University of California picked up nineteen Paloma graduates for five of its campuses: Berkeley (five), UCLA (eight), Riverside, Santa Barbara, and San Diego, with two each. Eight Paloma grads went to Ivy League schools, while three went to Stanford University and a prestigious Southern California consortium of colleges, and two went to traditionally black institutions. Most of the remaining students went directly on to selective, private universities spread across the United States, while two students went to a local community college and one went to the University of Colorado.

The Paloma counseling office was located on the second floor of the administration building. To reach this office from the front door, one had to walk up a staircase and down two corridors that were adorned with the class portraits of every woman ever sent forth from Paloma. It was hard to imagine students passing by this collection of decades of predecessors without drinking in the history of Paloma's role in the education of women, getting a sense of their pedigree, and quite possibly feeling empowered.

Mrs. Ball's sole job was to assist Paloma students in planning for and executing their college search process. Since Paloma was explicitly a college preparatory school, the college advising program was intense. "There's a lot of conversation about college around here all the time." All of Paloma's efforts were viewed through the lens of eventual college placement, from the ninth graders who were advised to take the biology achievement tests in June, because their course was geared toward that preparation, on through the rest of the courses, clubs, and school activities.

---

1. All quotes in this chapter are by the college counselor at the school cited.

Mrs. Ball's individual college counseling efforts however, do not begin until January of a student's junior year. Starting in September, she was besieged by students requesting achievement test taking advice and planning. Although the Dean of Studies helps each student plan her courses each academic year, Mrs. Ball is often informally consulted by students who requested her help about their course plans. Formal college advising, however, does not begin until January of the junior year. "There's a reason for that. For one thing, there's only one of me, and having to deal with the seniors is a pretty much full-time job."

By February, Mrs. Ball has not only begun the process anew with the current junior class but she has visited personally with every junior. During her counseling time, Mrs. Ball helps each student through every step, from planning and executing the college choice process to helping decide which admissions offers should be accepted. Some students

> come in here, bring the forms that have to be filled out, say good-bye, and that's sort of it. And some of them are here day in and day out. But I would imagine . . . that I have probably spent on an average of 10 to 15 hours actually with each kid.

When she first meets with a student, Mrs. Ball describes it as "a chat. . . . I don't want them to feel that they're under any pressure from me or from the school or whatever, and I tell them that this is sort of like a mock college interview." She asks each young woman if she has talked with her parents about college, if she has visited any colleges, if she has any older brothers and sisters or close friends who have influenced her thinking about college, and what "are you sort of thinking about, East Coast, West Coast, in between." Built into these series of questions is the assumption that not only are parents and friends important influences in this process, but also that they convey knowledge, attitudes, and expectations about college.

She is aware of the pressure inherent in the college choice process and keeps the conversation focused on "general things." She consciously never asks students about potential majors. Rather, she inquires as to whether they have any thoughts about what they are interested in.

> When you say the word "major" to a kid in high school . . . it's another one of those things that adds pressure . . . because they think that you're saying, "Tell me what you're going to do for the rest of your life," and that's not what I'm trying to do at all.

Because of the pressure on students about making college choices, Mrs. Ball is careful that her college counseling program maintain a balance between accurate and available information and emotional management.

> It's a real bind, because you want people to have as much information and help as they can possibly get. But sometimes here if you start talking

to them about college too early, it has a very bad effect. We deal with trying to keep their stress level down as much as possible anyway, and you mention college to some of these kids and especially parents and . . . it's like throwing up a red flag. So I try to really low-key everything that's formal.

All Paloma students are required to take the PSATs in the tenth grade, "for practice," and then take the SATs in their junior year. Occasionally a student, under the direction of her parents, will take the PSATs in the ninth grade. As Mrs. Ball characterizes it, "about one person out of every class will have been taking SAT since she was knee-high to a grasshopper."

Even more noteworthy is the fact that all Paloma students are explicitly and repeatedly encouraged to take achievement tests. The school expectation is for students to take achievement tests whenever they complete a class. Many Paloma courses are "very strong and the kids do really well on the test, so we encourage them to take it." Frequently, juniors take three achievement tests in June.

A piece of the Paloma strategy for having all students take the SATs and achievements is that approximately 75 percent of students apply to the UC system, even though the expressed purpose for many was as a backup. However, maybe about one-third of a class attends a UC. When applying to the UCs, a student can get in based on a combination of test scores and GPAs alone, and Paloma hopes that students' scores "will be high enough, and then they won't have to hassle with anything else."

In fact, students can oftentimes be so geared to the University of California requirements that they hound Mrs. Ball for advice at a fine level of detail. For example, students question her about whether they should "take the subject A exam for the UC system or . . . count on making a three on my advanced placement test?" Her approach to answering students is always to focus on the safe bet and remind students that there are no guarantees in terms of advanced placement or any other scores. Mrs. Ball is sometimes taken aback by the frequency and calculus of questions.

Mrs. Ball often suggests that students who are just beginning to think about their college options use

> Petersen's or the College Board software programs . . . that's kind of
> fun, especially for some of them who just don't know from nothin'
> what they're interested in or where they think they want to go. And
> they can come up and answer all the questions and get the whole list
> of schools, and then they start looking in the big book and then the
> catalogues and brochures.

After she visits with every student, Mrs. Ball's next interaction with juniors is "pretty informal . . . they'll be popping in to ask about classes to take for next year." Moreover, a lot of Paloma students visit colleges over spring vacation. Paloma has a school policy stating that a student can miss four days of school throughout her junior and senior years to visit colleges. However, students have to secure Mrs. Ball's permission to do it. "They have to come in and we talk about . . . where they've been . . . or where they're going, and then they come back and tell me what they thought."

In addition to Paloma students expecting and being expected to make a lot of college visits, Paloma assumes its students will attend programs at other preparatory schools. Paloma expects their students' participation in these types of educational experiences will help generally in the college preparation process, acquaint the student with college life, and introduce the students to being away from home.

> A lot of them visit schools . . . go to special summer kinds of programs . . . Andover, Exeter, and places like that...as a preview to see whether or not 'Yes!' They do want to go to school in the East. 'Yes!' They would be happy in a small liberal arts school. . . . A lot of them travel abroad. The Spanish teacher here takes a bunch of kids to Spain every year. . . . Last year the Latin teacher took them to Greece and the year before she took them to Italy.

Mrs. Ball sees her junior year efforts directed at both students *and* parents. She talks individually to not only the students but also parents; she met with one-third of the parents of this study's senior class. Also, Mrs. Ball develops and distributes a college handbook to each junior. She is quite explicit about the fact that parents need to talk clearly with their daughters about finances. In a cover letter that accompanies the college handbook, she asks parents to "talk eyeball-to-eyeball with your kid about money so that everybody's on the same wavelength about where you can afford to go to school."

That handbook also is distributed to students and parents, along with a copy of the student's transcript. Mrs. Ball believes the transcript is necessary "for realistic college planning." She is painfully aware of the admissions pressure her students face and tries to head off some parents' tendencies to escalate pressure. She hopes parents got the message.

> Don't make your kid apply to all the schools in the United States that have big names. Because maybe one or two rejection letters build character, but after that it's a pretty bad situation.

Mrs. Ball, at all times, shows extreme sensitivity to the pressures of admissions today. Her college counseling program is focused on doing all that she can to try to decrease admissions pressure. Her clear mission is "to protect these kids to some extent, and I don't want them applying to schools where they're just going to get zapped . . . It's not fair at all." Clearly, Paloma students receive this message and follow advice to apply to a majority of "safe" colleges. The average

Paloma student applies "to seven schools, she'd probably get into four or five of them." Mrs. Ball goes beyond an admissions management strategy and fosters a rejection management strategy.

Beyond her direct work with students, Mrs. Ball tries to make use of all of Paloma's resources in carrying out her college counseling and assistance functions. At the end of the academic year, she collects detailed information from all of the junior year teachers on each student's classroom performance so she can write the official school letter of recommendation.

She has an additional explicit goal in doing this: to get those teachers to write up the student's performance while it is still fresh in their minds. Thus, when the teachers are called upon by students to write letters of recommendation, they have this report to refer to. They will be able to write eloquently and in some detail about what that student's work was like, including any special research or projects the student completed, with the original enthusiasm the teacher may have experienced for that student.

> I give them back to the teachers, so that . . . they can have something that was fresh in their heads when they were actually teaching the kid.

When school starts back in the fall, Mrs. Ball meets with the seniors for about an hour to discuss "nuts and bolts," specifically taking the SAT again and achievements tests. "We ask them to sit for the English achievement . . . because they do very well on it."

Next comes the process of choosing where to apply to college. Mrs. Ball's major agenda at this point in the college choice process is to give the seniors information on recent Paloma graduates and how they fared in admissions processes at various colleges, given their grades and SAT scores.

> We get down to actually where are you applying, what are your chances of getting in. . . . These are the kinds of people who have applied to these schools before, these are the people who got in, this is how you fit into that picture. And I try to help them come up with a good group of schools. I want the kids who walk out of here to go to college and be happy where they are. And I don't care whether it's Harvard or Party State.

As egalitarian as this sentiment is, in fact, no one from Paloma applies to or attends Party State.

Mrs. Ball also is concerned with a second issue: to make it clear that Paloma does not get students admitted to college. Instead, it is the students' hard work and achievements that are responsible for successful admissions.

> When I first came here . . . the accusation was that the school didn't care about anybody except those kids who were getting in the pres-

tigious schools. And he [the former headmaster] had a favorite phrase, and that was "We got two into Stanford this year, we got seven into Harvard this year." And I kept saying "We didn't get anybody in anywhere.". . . The kids got in. The kids did the work. The kids filled out the applications . . . we are such a small part of the whole picture . . . give the credit where it's due, and it's due to them.

Mrs. Ball sees her job as empowering students and not the school. She believes this stance of giving students credit for the process and accomplishments, as well as her healthy attitude toward the whole college counseling process, is attributable to thirteen years' experience in college counseling and admissions, *and* to being "a good mother."

Mrs. Ball's knowledge of the admissions process is critical to Paloma's climate of providing expertise to help students make their own choices. "I've been doing this all my life, I mean for all intents and purposes . . . you can almost punch buttons and the information comes out of my mouth." However, she also is adamant about drawing a clear set of guidelines for parceling out what is the student's, the parent's, and her responsibility. Some mothers expect Mrs. Ball to do the work of researching and choosing appropriate colleges for their daughters.

That woman came in here last spring and she said, "Tell me a list of places where my kid can get into school." And I said, "I can give you a list, but I'm doing all the work and that's not my job. . . . This is part of your daughter's experience as much as taking English, or math, or whatever it is she's doing, and you all have got to bear some of this too.

A key element in most admissions applications is the school's letter of recommendation. In an another example of the time, attention, and dedication showered upon Paloma students, Mrs. Ball writes those letters

in the summertime between the junior and senior years, and I can spend as much as two to three hours on one of those letters. Again, it depends on how well I know the kid. . . . It's part of my job and I have a choice: I can either do it in the summer or I can try to do it in the fall.

Mrs. Ball sees her role in college counseling as spending a lot of time in the fall with students, holding their hands: "These kids are bright and they're sophisticated . . . but they still need a lot of stroking sometimes and I spend an awful lot of time doing that." When the college acceptances start coming in, Mrs. Ball spends a lot of time trying to help students decide what their best choice will be. She believes she is "very careful. I don't ever say to a kid, 'You ought to go to such-and-such a place.' I really want it to be her choice."

Mrs. Ball finds that her advising credibility is enhanced with students because she herself has visited many college campuses through the programs offered by many colleges to high school counselors.

> That is absolutely the most helpful thing that can happen to me, is to go and be on a college campus, and to talk with faculty and to talk to students, just like a kid . . . I love doing that because I feel like I learn so much from being in that environment and recognizing whether those would be the kind of places that our kids ought to go.

The visits enable her to say to students and parents, "When I was at that campus, this is what was going on. These are the kind of people that I talked to."

She has visited six schools in Oregon; most of the more selective, private California colleges; colleges in Ohio, such as Dennison, Ohio Wesleyan, College of Wooster, and Oberlin; and many others, including Cornell, Hobart and William Smith, Ithaca, St. Lawrence, Johns Hopkins, Bucknell, Franklin and Marshall, the University of Virginia, Washington and Lee, and William and Mary. Mrs. Ball sometimes combines school visits with professional meetings such as the National Association of College Admissions Counselors.

For a private school's profile or additional information on admissions prospects, Mrs. Ball relies a lot on a booklet from the California Association of Independent Colleges. "You want the data, you just pick it up, and there it is, and that's real clear information as far as I'm concerned." Mrs. Ball also develops a list of the prior year's Paloma graduates and where they were accepted to help students and parents in college choice decision making. This list displays all Paloma graduates (identified only by GPA), according to where they applied, their SAT scores, achievement scores, and whether or not they were admitted to a particular institution. This allows the college hopefuls to compare themselves to their immediate predecessors. Students said that looking at this compilation was pretty sobering.

Paloma has about sixty-five college representatives come through every fall. Students are given the schedule of college visits on a weekly basis, and each representative's visit is announced in Paloma's daily bulletin. Seniors are allowed to skip class to come to talk to these representatives, and the underclasswomen can come if they have a free period. "We have people from all over."

Mrs. Ball finds that Paloma young women are looking for colleges where they can receive "a basic liberal arts education." An occasional Paloma student wants to go into architecture or engineering, but mostly they "want to continue the same kinds of things that they've done here, just in a larger, different environment."

In terms of advising students on the "feel," the intangibles of campus environments, Mrs. Ball suggests students roam the campus

> read the graffiti in the bathrooms, look at the posters in the student union . . . see what the political climate is, or what the social tone

seems to be by what's being advertised. Go hang out in the student union or wherever people hang and see what they're talking about. . . . I just tell the kids to follow their guts. I don't know what else to tell them because I honestly believe that you can feel it . . . whether it's right for you or not.

Mrs. Ball links college "feel" to how a visitor might sense when she arrives at Paloma, "a certain feeling when you walked on this campus." She discussed Paloma's photographs of graduates as a lineage of people "who have been at this place" and suggested that it evokes a feeling of connection to the institution. She discussed how the seventh and eighth graders were often fascinated by the photographs and sometimes made up stories about what a particular graduate was like, based only on her photograph.

Mrs. Ball voiced a concern with trying to build on the Paloma junior high experience. About half of the students who enter Paloma in the seventh grade stay on, while the rest enter in the ninth grade. Currently, the school would like their retention rates to be higher, and they are "trying to do something about that."

All of the Paloma curriculum is "pretty standardized" and Mrs. Ball tries to impress upon students that they should not be concerned about how a particular course will "look" to an admissions officer, that admissions people will be more concerned with what the students are learning, and that they "be consistent and that they be persistent. And that's the message that I try to get across to them."

Paloma's curriculum is a part of the college counseling program and climate. In junior English classes, students work on essay development by completing the "Common Application," especially, the essay portion. This form has been developed by 117 participating private colleges and the National Association of Secondary School Principals. Paloma students

write the essay, turn it into their English teacher, the teacher's going to grade it, help them improve it, that sort of thing, and I will have that included in their files that I have here in my office. And when they come back to school in the fall I'll give it back to them, and it is amazing to see what happens when they get those back.

Mrs. Ball believes that during the junior year the whole college choice process is not very real to students. They watch their older friends going through "this college business," the anxiety of getting in, the acceptances, and then the anxiety of trying to decide where to go. In September, their perspectives and motivations change.

Thus, junior year exercises, like filling out the Common Application essay, are "kind of a game." When students review it in their senior year they say

'God, I did a lousy job on this!' Or 'I can't believe I wrote that badly! What could I have been thinking about?' So you know, in a sense it's next to an exercise in futility, because most of them don't use it for anything. But in another sense, they get it and they realize how serious things are. It's real in the fall.

Because it is a college preparatory school, everyone and everything at Paloma is geared toward college preparation, "just by nature . . . Everybody's interested in the college process. Most people are as helpful as they can absolutely positively be." Mrs. Ball described the plight of one student who was trying to decide between Williams and Harvard. She recalled walking around campus and at different points in time various staff and faculty were talking to this student, lending whatever personal and counseling assistance they could.

> The first person I saw her talking to this morning was a faculty member who has a daughter who went to Princeton and another one who went to Harvard. . . . the next person I saw talking to her is another faculty member whose ex-husband was on the faculty at Harvard. . . . So I think that everybody here on the faculty is involved in the counseling part of all this business.

Extracurricular activities are extensive at Paloma, and everyone knows they help build college application potential. Paloma offers sports, drama, cultural clubs, language clubs, and service groups like hunger projects, an adopt-a-grandparent group, and Amnesty International.

> As much as we possibly can, many of us on the faculty encourage the kids to do some kind of community service, because they need to know that there's another world other than Paloma School and the kind of social circles they travel in.

Another part of Mrs. Ball's job is to help students, once accepted, winnow their list of possible college destinations to something reasonable. Yet a frustration she experiences is that this process occurs at the same time of year as her meetings with juniors, who are beginning their college choice process.

> I find myself having to switch gears all the time . . . all the stuff is in for these kids [seniors] now, move on to the juniors. Fresh breath, fresh air, let's go. A new meet. And the seniors are still here. They're still on my doorstep, they're still on the chairs, they're still stopping me, "Got a question for you." . . . That's fine, I'm glad to be where I can help them. But sometimes I think "My God, are they never going to go away?" Because I have just set my mind that it's time to start anew.

Because of the overlap in the needs of college-bound seniors and juniors, Mrs. Ball "begs" the students to get "everything in by about the first of December . . . for the most part they'll do pretty much what you ask them to do." In spite of the hecticness of this time, Mrs. Ball believes the pressure cooker is at maximum capacity while seniors wait for acceptances and rejections.

> Probably the worst times are in March and April. See, the UCs send out letters beginning in March and a lot of kids get admitted and that's great. That first letter is the greatest relief in the world. And then that slows down and then there's nothing until around the first of April. And there's a lot of gnashing of teeth and pulling of hair.

Fifty out of the fifty-six Paloma seniors ended up in the real struggle of trying to decide which offers to accept. After reminding them about the prior September, when they were "scared to death they weren't going to get in anywhere," Mrs. Ball then asks

> You've got five places to choose from, all of which are really desirable for you and right for you. There's the situation you're in. Aren't you embarrassed by your riches?"...You've never been allowed to make a major decision in your life and now you have to make one. How are you going to handle it?

Mrs. Ball is concerned about the many adults in students' lives who help escalate the pressure on seniors. In this class, one senior was being pressured by Paloma alumnae to go to their college alma mater, Williams College. These alumnae bought this Paloma senior an airline ticket to visit Williams. After the trip, she was as enthusiastic about Williams as she was about Harvard. But she then had to try to figure out what to do and where to go. Mrs. Ball's concern was that these behaviors are like the highly publicized efforts colleges use to recruit top athletes, a misdirection of aid and resources. She would like to see this kind of aid be need-based.

> They're putting pressure on her.... I said to her, "Now you just remember when you take that airline ticket and go to Williams how you feel about those athletes."...She got the point...I think aid money should go first to the kid who really needs it.

As a matter of fact, Mrs. Ball believes that pressure from parents and other adults is misguided and distorting.

> If I ruled the world, if I were the goddess, I would remove the part of parents' and other adults' brains that enables them to talk about colleges with seniors in high school. The whole senior year. I think it would help a lot.

She is concerned with what she sees and with what some students articulate: that parents, oftentimes fathers more than mothers, are too invested in their daughters' college destinations. Mrs. Ball attributes this to a competitive urge and a need to prove something. As one student said to Mrs. Ball:

My mother is real mellow about it. She wants me to go to school where I'm going to be happy. Sometimes I get the impression my father wants the stickers to go on the back end of the car.

Mrs. Ball perceives Paloma parental involvement in the college choice process as quite high: "That's why a lot of them have their kids here." Parents do not usually ask to discuss college with Mrs. Ball until the eleventh grade, but some come in when their daughters are sophomores. More often, the early visits were from parents

> who are first-generation Americans and haven't been through this system . . . because they're nervous and they don't know what to expect and . . . the newspapers always have horror stories about people who don't get in. . . . they know they can come in and talk to me if they want to . . . Some of them are scared.

Mrs. Ball also is concerned about conveying her expertise to parents, and she strives to make parents aware early on about her credentials as a college admissions counselor. She is aware that because these parents are paying high, private school tuition and because they are concerned that their daughters get into "good" colleges, they want a college counselor who is an admissions authority with experience in selective admissions.

> It helps tremendously, because they recognize that I know what I'm talking about, that I didn't just blow in off the street. I will even sometimes, particularly with parents to establish my authority, say I worked in an admissions office where the ratio for out-of-state students was 10 to 1—we had 6,000 applicants for 600 places and, that kind of routine, and then they can see that yeah, hey, maybe she does know what she's talking about.

Financial aid does not play much of a role in how Paloma students choose colleges, according to Mrs. Ball. An occasional student is concerned about the financial aid package that is offered, but maintains an excited and positive face in front of friends. In one particular case, a student from a single parent family consulted privately with Mrs. Ball about her monetary concerns.

> I didn't want to tell you in front of them, but the financial aid people have offered me $10,000. And I said 'That's great. Can you make it with that?' And she said that they think they can.

Mrs. Ball could not remember a single case in this particular graduating class of a student coming in to request a financial aid form (FAF). She claims that either the family had decided to attend a UC "because it costs about as much as it does to go here as a day student, or they're so well-fixed that it's all taken care of."

Mrs. Ball has limited knowledge of financial aid but feels that, given the socioeconomic profile of Paloma's students, she does not need to know much more than

> Here is an FAF, this is what this does . . . colleges will take into consideration the fact that the price of real estate here is so inflated when they do your needs assessment . . . I don't really know much about it.

To summarize, the college counseling functions are the centerpiece of Paloma's college preparatory efforts. College guidance is omnipresent: Mrs. Ball, teacher interactions, and course content are all directed at supporting college choice planning. Moreover, Mrs. Ball ensures that Paloma's approach is proactive; she meets with students individually, at length, if necessary, to discuss their plans and options. A particularly important mission of Mrs. Ball's college counseling program is to be as supportive as possible with these students, to be aware of the competitive admissions environment they are facing, and to help buffer them from the expectations of their families and other adults.

Gate of Heaven High School

"Good Morning" softly, gently eased into the room, seemingly coming from nowhere. The woman's voice was warm and reassuring, offering a prelude to the morning prayer, as she prefaced her Bible reading with a note that this passage would be read from a female perspective, since this was an all-girls high school. She then began:

> Then Jesus said to his disciples, "I tell you solemnly, it will be hard for a rich woman to enter the kingdom of heaven. Yes, I tell you again, it is easier for a camel to pass through the eye of a needle than for a rich woman to enter the kingdom of heaven." (Matthew 19: 23–26)

Startled out of my preoccupation with college choice processes, I reflected on beginning a school day with prayer and contemplation, and on the specifics of the prayer's subtle message discouraging wealth and whether that extended to certain successes. The Modern Catholic Dictionary says of wealth "riches of themselves do not help to gain eternal salvation, but are rather an obstacle to salvation."

Gate of Heaven High School has been providing Catholic women's education for over 134 years, since its founding in 1854 by an order of Catholic nuns from Ireland. The total enrollment at Gate of Heaven High School was 450, 117 of whom were seniors. Gate of Heaven is a private school and, as such, charges an annual tuition of $2,500. A little less than one-tenth of this year's seniors received financial aid. Although it is a private school, with most families meeting the tuition charges without help, the majority of Gate of Heaven students are from lower income and lower middle class families. At the time of this study, a slim majority of Gate of Heaven students were white and 43 percent were people of color.

According to the counseling staff, 95 percent of Gate of Heaven graduates go directly on to college after graduation. Sixty percent of seniors go on to four-year colleges, while 35 percent attend community colleges. Gate of Heaven High School is located in a metropolitan area, which is among the fifteen largest U. S. cities. It is surrounded by a lower middle class residential neighborhood and a major Catholic university. The school consists of a single large building, a tar yard, and a parking lot along two sides. On the bottom floor is the cafeteria, the Dean of Students Office, and the student gathering and hangout area. It has several vending machines, the scene of "carbo-loading" during morning and afternoon breaks.

A grand entrance hall, accessible from the street, is located on the first floor, as are classrooms, a computer lab, and the principal's and other administrators' offices. The first-floor hallway sports a display case that includes honors and awards received by the school and staff, as well as a book on death and dying, which features a chapter written by the Dean of Students. The second floor is completely devoted to classrooms, while the third floor is predominantly comprised of classrooms and counseling quarters. The counseling offices are tucked away in a corner on the top floor at the rear of the building. The entryway houses the secretary's desk. In this space are posters featuring California College of Arts and Crafts, City College, American College in Paris, and College of San Mateo. Down a small corridor are the offices of the counselors and the school nurse. There are little slips of paper on which students can request appointments with the counselors, along with a little wicker basket on the wall outside of each counselors' office for students to deposit the appointment slips.

At the end of the corridor is the inner sanctum, the Career Center. It is a large room with many posters, books, tables, and chairs. One bookshelf is devoted solely to University of California catalogs, promotional materials, and applications, while another is devoted exclusively to California State Universities. A third shelf is devoted to California private schools, while the remaining two and one-half shelves are devoted to schools in other parts of the United States, with over eighty books per shelf. The books range from individual college catalogs to *Peterson's Guide to College* and the *College Handbook* to an *Index of Majors*. Scattered throughout the room are career pamphlets on forestry, music, dance, and fashion.

The college posters that dot the walls include UC Riverside, Oregon State, Willamette, Mills College, West Point, Adelphi, Spelman, UC Berkeley, Western Oregon State, College of Santa Fe, College of Mary, Marymount College (NY), University of Utah, New York University, St. Martin's College, U. S. Air Force Academy, College of Notre Dame, and Northeastern, and a "No Drugs" poster.

Featured prominently in front of the entry doorway are three large bulletin board displays. One is a hand-drawn, enlarged California map with every public and private college marked by a small flag. A second display is a National Association of College Admissions Counselors United States map. The final bulletin board is entitled "Financial Aid Is Gold" and contains information about deadlines and the availability of financial aid for meeting college expenses.

Gate of Heaven High School has three counselors for a student body of 450: two academic counselors and a college counselor. Each academic counselor advises two full grades, ninth and tenth and eleventh and twelfth. The college counselor focuses exclusively on college preparation, working primarily with the eleventh and twelfth grades. A student meets with a counselor an average of four times during the academic year.

Ms. Trent, the college counselor, is the daughter of a Princeton-educated college professor and a Vassar-educated special education teacher. She attended a small, private college in Illinois directly after high school but soon dropped out. Eventually, she attended several community colleges and completed her bachelor's degree at Antioch University's Independent Learning Center. She has worked at Gate of Heaven for two years as the college counselor. Outside of school, she and a group of colleagues operate a fledgling, non-profit, college counseling organization.

At Gate of Heaven, the college counseling process begins in the ninth grade. Counselors consciously try not to overload the students, and the information they offer is focused only on necessities, while advisement is focused on career planning and developing a four-year curricular plan.

> What we do is, we try not to overwhelm them too much in ninth grade. One of the things that we're really aware of is that if they don't start planning ahead they end up not doing well in classes in ninth grade; then they're tracked out of classes in tenth grade . . . They sit down with their counselor and they develop a four-year course plan, so that they know what they're going to take each year.

The counseling staff organizes an annual college night, with a representative from the community college system, the CSU and UC systems, and the private college sector. They also hold an annual financial aid workshop and a biannual career fair, where "about 100 women come from traditional and nontraditional areas."

Gate of Heaven offers each ninth-grade student individual appointments, career testing, and general academic ability standardized testing, which emphasizes identifying each student's strengths and weaknesses. In addition, all Gate of Heaven freshmen attend small group guidance sessions

> with six to ten students, where we . . . talk about colleges in a very beginning kind of way . . . helping them visualize what college is like, because they don't have any idea. So instead of cramming them with information and deadlines and checklists, we're saying: What do you think it would be like? What would a dormitory be like? What would

it be like having a roommate? How do you picture a college campus, do you expect a wall around it? How do you think students would dress?

For tenth graders, Gate of Heaven offers another college night and a career and college planning guide developed by a neighboring county's Office of Education. In developing its college counseling program, the counseling staff does not make any assumptions that students know anything about college. All tenth-grade students are required to "hear at least three college reps, so we have representatives come from many colleges." Sophomores, in their college guidance discussions, focus on

> what the difference between a state and a UC is, and . . . talking more about what are the differences between a community college, between vocational programs and academic programs.

Gate of Heaven counselors provide sophomores with more standardized testing, to assess how students' scores have changed from the previous year, and additional career testing, through the "Major/Minor Finder," which helps high school students pick a potential college major and minor. The counseling staff also lets Gate of Heaven students know about other kinds of work opportunities "apprenticeship programs and internships, Explorers Club, things like that where they get more career information."

In the beginning of their junior year, Gate of Heaven students fill out a college career questionnaire designed to give Ms. Trent an initial sense of each student's college expectations. The questionnaire asks, "Are you planning to go to college? If so, where? Do you know what the requirements are? Have you discussed this with your parents?"

Ms. Trent has developed a college planning achievement award book for eleventh- and twelfth-grade students. If students complete eight out of ten of the listed tasks, they get an award at the end of the school year.

> They're really simple things . . . making an appointment with your counselor, visit a college rep, know your PSAT score by heart, know your GPA, really simple stuff.

The book concludes, in a nonjudgmental fashion, with three ranges of things a student can do to prepare for college. First, the minimum expectations for college preparation are offered for those students who have extensive work and family obligations. An average range of expectations is detailed, followed by the maximum expectations for college preparation, targeted at those students who "want to do everything, and [for whom] college is real important."

During the junior year, small-group discussions focus on "the next stage of college counseling," picking classes for the senior year, information about vocational schools, and discussions about different types of colleges. Based on information from the questionnaires, students are assigned to counselor-led, focused discussion groups. All students who are uncertain of their plans are in one group, while students interested in UCs, CSUs, and community colleges are in groups to "talk about all the programs that are available . . . and to . . . [cluster] groups of students who have similar interests."

Gate of Heaven students are well-informed about community-based college preparatory events such as the major college fair at the city's civic auditorium and the college night at the nearby Jesuit boys high school. Gate of Heaven also has a monthly calendar of events and ongoing presentations about college and careers.

A few years ago, Gate of Heaven instituted a program to have a college guidance student representative for each homeroom in the eleventh and twelfth grades. This representative

> gets up and reads announcements about college stuff. So maybe it's to
> say that a certain rep is coming, or it's to say that there's a career fair
> or there's a scholarship.

Ms. Trent actively recruits students of color for these positions "so that they have that visibility and that chance to get up and speak." The students selected to serve in this capacity are specifically *not* "the typical superstars." The school evaluates each homeroom's students and designates a student who "has seemed really motivated and interested in school but has been a low-profile student."

At Gate of Heaven, the college counselor and academic counselor meet individually with each student every year.

> By the time they are a junior or a senior, they meet with their acad-
> emic counselor twice a year and with their college counselor at least
> once or twice a year. And those are the bare minimum; there are very
> few students I only see twice a year or the academic counselor only
> sees twice a year.

In the senior year, contact with the counseling staff escalates: "I alone see the student probably three times . . . the academic counselor probably sees them three to four times." Students fill out another questionnaire to provide the counseling staff with information on who needs help. The form is differentiated for those students going to a two-year or four-year college. "We use that to kind of get an idea of who's really lost and to see those students first."

Ms. Trent sees as an important part of her job getting Gate of Heaven students to stretch their horizons by looking at private schools and out-of-state schools because

> we think that their decision making process in spite of everything we
> do, is very herdlike, that they're just following the crowds, and like cat-
> tle all going to UC and state, and we want them to be brave enough
> to look at other things.

Only 15 percent of Gate of Heaven students attend private colleges, while 2 percent go out-of-state. Occasionally, Ms. Trent's efforts to encourage students to break out of traditional college destinations pay off. She has photocopied articles from popular news magazine about the benefits of attending traditionally black and women's colleges. In the prior graduating class, a charismatic African American senior decided to attend a black college and helped Ms. Trent to encourage other students to follow her lead.

> Last year was our first year we got a lot of black students to go to black colleges in the South . . . It was a lot her charisma that they just really got into that . . . So they were getting some support from the school, plus they were having a peer who was really leading them to do that.

Much as Ms. Trent has tried to encourage Gate of Heaven students to consider applying to women's colleges, she has been unsuccessful because of the young women's strong desire to interact with young men and because of the fear of being labeled a lesbian.

> They think the people are going to think they're a lesbian or something. If you go to a women's college there's got to be something wrong with you.

Most students do not seem to be able to make the kind of college choice that deviates from the mainstream.

Choosing a women's college is a different decision than choosing to go to a women's high school. For most students, their parents made the choice for them to attend Gate of Heaven because, as Ms. Trent expresses it, the public high schools were seen as "dens of iniquity and . . . their parents think that their kids will be protected by going here." Now the choice is the student's, and Ms. Trent found in her discussions with students that

> it's a different thing out of your own free choice to go to a school that's going to—cost more money, that's going to be more women, all women—why would you want to do it—why would you spend more money to go to a women's college? There're many good reasons, but none that they agree with.

Without understanding it, Ms. Trent said she thought African American students found it was easier and more acceptable to attend a traditionally black college than for any of Gate of Heaven's young women to attend a women's college.

Gate of Heaven students "really don't consider" private schools or out-of-state schools; they are "generally overwhelmed by all the choices." The high-achieving students have heard of and will occasionally apply to Ivy League or other prestigious schools. Ms. Trent also pointed out that students who have spent a portion of their life in another geographical area will think about attending other state schools—attractive party schools, like schools in Hawaii. Ms. Trent finds there is always a small, avant garde contingent who considers international schools: "There's got to be a little glamour attached and mystique attached, or there's got to be some personal experience with it."

Every spring, the counseling staff distributes a form for students to complete, asking where they have been accepted. Because of time and resource limitations, the information is filed away but not reviewed by the staff. The only records kept are those where students have accepted admission offers. Thus, Ms. Trent does not always know if the students who have exotic college considerations followed through and received applications, applied, or had been accepted. For all students, she sees

> once they're accepted, something happens where they opt for the safer choice, the school that's closer to home, that's most familiar, that's most endorsed by their friends.

Large numbers of Gate of Heaven students end up attending the local CSU campus—San Francisco State—or the local community college—San Francisco City College.

> I even try to get them to go to other community colleges besides City College. College of San Mateo is very fashionable to go to . . . and then there're some tougher kids who say, "Well, City College is in my neighborhood and I'm going to go there," and I say "Well you know, you can go to Skyline and College of San Mateo (CSM), and maybe Skyline and CSM might be smaller and more of a new experience," "No, no, the bus is right here, City College."

Each year, Ms. Trent finds most students go to college where their friends go, and each year there is at least one "hot" college. "For some reason, CSU at Long Beach is fashionable. . . . They really don't know anything about Long Beach." Another school, located near the ocean, often considered by students is San Diego State "and it just connotes parties, sunshine, surfer. . . ." Ms. Trent finds that the difficult part of her job is to try not to discourage students' aspirations, but to help them be realistic. She is aware that students see pushing realism as a "parental downer trip." She tries to have the parents of the previous year's seniors come in to talk about their daughters' experiences at their schools.

> The parents will say "We're spending all this money for our daughter to be down there . . . She can only get into two classes.". . . they [the Gate of Heaven students] just don't want to hear it.

Ms. Trent finds that even though the counseling program tries to introduce college choice processes throughout the high school years, there is a senior year crescendo of fear and pressure.

> It's really hard no matter how much we try to provide a kind of grad-
> uated approach of looking at a little more each year, there's kind of a
> pitch of hysteria that happens senior year where there's a sudden sense
> of deadlines, of things that are required.

Gate of Heaven students average three applications. However, Ms. Trent
finds that during the senior year, students still procrastinate about choosing a particular college.

> They're more panicked this year because each state application costs
> forty-five dollars. Before they thought they would just apply to all
> nineteen and they wouldn't have to make a decision. Then they're fig-
> uring out how many hundreds of dollars that'll cost . . . the message
> that I try to give is "know something about the school you're apply-
> ing to and have some sense you'd be happy to go there." It just gets
> lost.

Ms. Trent finds that Gate of Heaven students are relatively unsophisticated
about the process of thinking about different colleges and choosing among them.
She said that when they go to college fairs they

> go around like zombies with their little plastic bag they've been given
> that they can just throw . . . catalogs into . . . they're too embarrassed
> to ask what GPA or SAT [is needed for admission].

She attributes this to their lack of consumerism.

The counseling staff tries to provide links between Gate of Heaven and as
many outside schools and programs as possible, including programs for the non-
college-bound student, offered by the public school system. Those students

> leave school a couple of periods early and they take a bus down to the
> school . . . and they're able to take vocational kinds of classes there and
> it's a fairly demanding program.

For the academically advanced Gate of Heaven student, there are programs
established so juniors and seniors can take classes at the local community college.
"If they want extra honors classes they can take a college-level class and it will
count as an honors and increase their GPA." There are periodic problems with
the arrangements, and often after being accepted, the only available classes are offered during Gate of Heaven's school day. However, Ms. Trent believes that even
this experience is useful. "They find out at least the experience of going to a college campus and what registration is like."

Gate of Heaven offers additional programs that coordinate with the local
UC campus, allowing a limited number of students to take classes and participate
in a summer talent development program for freshmen and sophomores. Ms. Trent

also encourages Gate of Heaven students to participate in independent educational programs, including one that is designed for students from underrepresented groups to learn about corporate America. The program includes an internship, with the ultimate goal to help students graduate from college and secure a job in the corporation for which they have interned.

In the senior year, workshops are offered on filling out financial aid forms, UC applications, and CSU applications, writing application essays, and selecting a college, though "very few students show up." Ms. Trent says she is lucky to have four or five seniors out of a class of 117 show up. This disappointing turnout is commonplace, extending to college nights where very few students or parents show up. Actually, Ms. Trent's expectations have shifted, so when thirty parents and students attend, she and the other Gate of Heaven staff are happy. To make these workshops more appealing to parents, sessions on coping with daughters who do not want to go to college and sessions on parenting issues are offered.

> Some years we've required parents to come and we felt like we should throw in something else for parents who maybe had tons of kids go to college already and knew everything on that.

Gate of Heaven attempts to build personal links between alumnae and seniors by having graduates come back to talk about their colleges. Ms. Trent, however, is keenly aware of the emotional pitfalls of that strategy.

> It's been a little tricky to get freshmen to come right back . . . they've got almost a kind of angry feeling . . . an aggressiveness. Maybe they're disenchanted by a UC and they thought that it would be wonderful, and they go over there and they find out that there are long lines for everything, and it wasn't what they expected. Or maybe they go to a community college and they're waiting for a counselor to call them and no counselor ever called them and they realize they have to do it all on their own.

For those students who have been away from Gate of Heaven for a longer period of time, Ms. Trent finds "it's harder to entice them to come to the school and talk."

Gate of Heaven seniors often are not ready to hear about certain aspects of college, especially about the transition from the known to the unknown.

> It's very frightening and they've gone to school together for sometimes twelve years . . . it's very intimidating for them to even come to a workshop or a group about making the transition.

Ms. Trent tries to make workshops more palatable and less threatening by talking about concrete things like, "How do you do your laundry at college?" Even so, attendance is poor.

Gate of Heaven mails information directly to parents for all workshops and information sessions it sponsors. However, parental involvement and attendance is low, and Ms. Trent attributes this to parents having very good intentions but

> a lot of people are just tired, or they're working in the evening, or they're single parents. . . . they hope that their daughter's getting the information at school . . . I think that there's some feeling that 'Well, you're going to a private school, the private school's going to take care of this for you, therefore we don't need to be involved in this.'

Ms. Trent adopted as her own, Gate of Heaven's special institutional mission—creating a truly supportive and multicultural environment for its diverse student body. She brings in speakers from advocacy groups for people of color to address students on educational advancement issues. Aside from the substantive content of these seminars, Gate of Heaven endeavors to bring in speakers who are themselves people of color to counterbalance Gate of Heaven's all-white faculty and give students exposure to people of color as role models. Ms. Trent also tries to inform students about educational opportunities and scholarships targeted for both specific minority groups and those addressed to a broad range of minorities. "Sometimes they think of a minority as that group over there, or they'll think if they're Asian that they're not an underrepresented minority."

Twice a year, Gate of Heaven counselors write and distribute a newsletter for seniors and another newsletter for parents of seniors about college opportunities and financial aid. The Gate of Heaven college guidance office is chock-full of scholarship information, which students constantly inquire about. The problem, as Ms. Trent perceives it, is that "something happens" so students never quite get around to pursuing financial aid. Therefore, she set up a financial aid corner in the career center, with one parent volunteer to "help students look up different schools or programs or scholarships." The Career Center parent volunteers are all mothers who come in once a week, after being trained to assist students in using the career center. The volunteers are available to all students, but most frequently they see tenth-, eleventh-, and twelfth-grade students. Volunteers administer individual career tests if students need them.

Gate of Heaven makes computers and software available to help students in the college search process. The software is installed in the first-floor computer lab machines, and there is always someone in the lab assisting students with generating a list of colleges that meet their criteria. Ms. Trent believes the process of operating the college search software is itself a learning experience. Sometimes students learn that a small college consists of approximately 5,000 to 10,000 students, compared to their small Catholic high school of 400-plus students. Ms. Trent believes that playing with the college choice software "gets them to think a little bit."

She also believes that her counseling responsibilities include getting students to think concretely about their options. She often tries to get students to make hypothetical decisions (while acknowledging that students may not be ready to make a final decision) to see what results will follow. Then she probes to see if the student is comfortable with her decision. She witnesses the advantages of forcing students to explicate their desires "because often they'll pick such selective criteria that they come up with only one school." Other students realize they need to narrow their criteria.

The software helps students get beyond thinking that only UC and state schools are affordable, guides students who do not have the first idea of how to research colleges, and directs students who are afraid to look at faraway colleges because they seem so remote. The software helps students think ideally about what they want in a college, as just a "starting off place." Ms. Trent informs her students that by doing this research on colleges, they will discover other decisions and choices. An advantage to using the software is that students get accustomed to making decisions and anticipating consequences.

Sometimes, Ms. Trent finds it difficult to deal with unrealistic student choices. She is afraid to come down hard on students, for fear that they may not come back to her; she does not want to lose an opportunity to help them sort through their options. Simultaneously, she is concerned with not shirking her responsibilities, just to keep students comfortable. Gate of Heaven requires all students to take the PSATs in eleventh grade. Ms. Trent offers an orientation session to explain the PSATs to students and another session to explain the test results. Although Gate of Heaven once offered an SAT coaching class, the experience was unsatisfactory because few students signed up for it. Ms. Trent and other school leaders discovered that a number of other high schools had established track records of providing SAT coaching classes, and more importantly, Gate of Heaven students preferred to take those SAT coaching classes with boys during the summer, when Gate of Heaven is not in session.

Gate of Heaven did not always require all students to take the PSATs. As a requirement though, some students feel coerced into paying for testing they do not want and feel that poor test results lower their self-esteem. Teachers express concern with bringing the school's overall average down by forcing all students to take the test, especially the academically less able. During Ms. Trent's tenure as a college counselor, she "insisted that everybody take it, because I felt like students change their minds . . . and I just felt it didn't hurt for them to take it and see how they did."

Ms. Trent experiences occasional frustration over trying to convince students that financial aid is available to them and that scholarships are not just for smart kids. She finds that Asian students do not perceive themselves as an underrepresented minority, while African American students think that scholarships are for high-achieving students. White students think scholarships are available only to ethnic minorities. In repeated financial aid workshops, Ms. Trent covers all pertinent information, only to have students say, "Yeah, but when my brother applied he didn't get anything." She said at that point she "just limps away," feeling that her credibility with the students has been "blown."

According to Ms. Trent, approximately one college representative a week comes to Gate of Heaven during the fall, approximately twenty or twenty-five college representatives total. On occasion, East Coast college representatives travel through the area and schedule an evening event at one of the downtown hotels, inviting Gate of Heaven students. Ms. Trent finds that this is not a particularly effective method of reaching Gate of Heaven students. She feels

> it's kind of crazy to expect that the students who won't get out of a class and come upstairs in the same building to go to a college rep's talk . . . are not about to go, take a bus into the business district, go to the Westin Hotel, and sit and talk with a rep from an East Coast college.

Gate of Heaven's college counseling environment is proactive, providing information and alternatives to students at all levels. It is a multifaceted approach, using teachers, discussion groups, and individual appointments to supplement guidebooks, software, and exercises. Moreover, Gate of Heaven's college counseling program's strategy is self-consciously educational and supportive. Possibly most important for these working-class students is that college guidance starts early and without presumptions of knowledge of college types, prerequisites, or strategies. From ninth grade through twelfth grade, students participate in a college guidance program of increasing complexity, which culminates in informed individual decision making supported by the school.

University High School

Situated at the corner of a busy intersection bordered by a small, upscale shopping center and residential area, University High School is a sprawling, suburban campus with many resources, buildings, and well-tended playing fields. The students dress fashionably in clothes from Benetton, The Gap, or The Limited, or sport the latest in all-black ensembles, with punkish hairstyles and pale makeup. The faculty and staff are well-credentialed, the best a high school can offer. Competition for getting a teaching job in this district is tough. UHS's libraries, science laboratories, and other technical facilities also are among the best available, particularly at a public secondary institution.

The main building houses the University High School administrative offices. Upon entering the Counseling and Guidance Office, a visitor sees spacious waiting and meeting areas, as well as comfortable counselors' offices. The connecting hall between the Guidance Office and the Career Center is complete with a laser disk player for students to experience the automated viewbooks sent by colleges; an Apple IIe computer, with software from *Peterson's Guide to Colleges* which students can use to generate a list of colleges to consider; VCR machines and tapes; and many free college catalogs.

The Career Center has four resource areas: a travel section symbolized by an overstuffed suitcase, a study section symbolized by books, a military section captured by a person saluting, and finally a career area that displays a hammer and nail. The walls are filled with posters such as "Keep your choices open, your dreams alive," another poster lists the choice colleges in America, and others include the "College Finder II Map" of the United States, and the "Selective Accredited Colleges and Major Universities" map, as well as posters from community colleges, foreign study programs, and summer study opportunities.

University High School has a well-deserved national reputation for academic excellence. UHS has been a California Distinguished School and a National Secondary School Recognition Program winner. Students apply "to everything in the book." Annually, 88 percent of graduates go directly to college, and 65 percent of those alumni go to four-year institutions. Of the 421 students in this graduating class, 51 percent are attending University of California campuses, 23 percent are attending California community colleges, 14 percent are attending California State University schools, and 12 percent are attending private schools in California.

The guidance program at University High School is structured so each of the four counselors is assigned to an entering class and works with that class throughout their high school career. Counseling at UHS, as in all California high schools, has been "thinned out" since Proposition 13, a budget-slashing initiative. The average counseling load during this study was one counselor for 367 students, whereas prior to Proposition 13 it was one counselor per 200 students. As the entering classes get smaller, the UHS counselors do not get better counseling loads or more time with individual students. Instead, the counselor of the freshman class is employed as a counselor three-fifths of the time while the sophmore class counselor is employed as a counselor four-fifths of the time. To make up a full-time load, those counselors teach classes in English or other academic specialties which, in the words of the senior class counselor "is a terrible way to go. They're just totally different roles. You can't do both well."

Matt Dix is the counselor for this University High School senior class. He is an alumnus of Johns Hopkins (BA), Stanford University (MA), and Santa Clara University (MA). He was a teacher for twenty years before switching to counseling. The UHS guidance program of assigning a counselor to a class means the counselor only works on college admissions every fourth year. Theoretically, this system allows for continuity in the development of relationships between each counselor and the students in his caseload: "I see them individually all the way through." In reality though, Mr. Dix *only* sees those students who come to him and sees them for two to three visits, totaling about forty-five minutes.

> They don't all come in obviously. Sometimes I'll spend more time, that's probably a decent average. Sometimes they'll bring a parent, sometimes they won't.

Moreover, because Mr. Dix was the counselor for the class during all of the students' high school years, he dealt with many other counseling needs in addition to college advising. He estimated that the balance between general guidance and college planning

> shifts a lot. Of course, now that I'm into the senior year I think the main percent of what I'm doing right now is college counseling. Last year I would guess the ratio was probably closer to 50 percent, and in the years of the ninth and tenth grade it was probably more like 30 percent or 40 percent.

Mr. Dix begins college counseling with his students in their freshman and sophomore years. Career planning is not part of the college counseling process as Mr. Dix defines it: he does not talk with students about what they might want to do after college. He advises them generally about courses to take in high school and about UC requirements.

> It really in a sense begins with their freshman year . . . you're talking in very vague terms with the freshmen and sophomores about UC requirements. . . . Initially of course everybody's going to at least a UC if not Harvard.

Beginning in the junior year the college counseling program gets more specific, and a hierarchy of futures available to students are laid out with certain options obviously foreclosed.

> You start having to get a little more specific because by that time the kids have track records, and especially with the UC and Cal State systems where it's only the sophomore and junior years that count, by the time you're midway in your junior year you're beginning to realize that certain things are no longer possible.

Initially, Mr. Dix talks with students about the college admissions process. He then discusses how to choose the right college and eventually gives students sample listings of colleges. He recommends that students consult Fisk's *Selective Guide to Colleges*.

> I go into the junior classes two or three times during the year, talking about taking the PSAT, talking about how they might make college choices, giving them some samples of listings from college guides just to show how they're written up and where they can go to find them.

For Mr. Dix, and apparently University High School, where "the majority of kids will go to either a UC or Cal State," there is a college advising baseline.

I usually begin looking at those two, and see what their possibilities are, and the kids invariably want to apply to UC whether they're planning to go there or not, just as either in some cases as a backup and other cases it's an unreachable goal.

In the case of private colleges, Mr. Dix generally recommends that students take four years of solid academic subjects to remain competitive.

The private schools are all so different that I don't get really tightly into details there other than to make general recommendations to kids that clearly if you're headed for a competitive college you'd better have four years of all of the solid subjects. And that's a pretty safe recommendation.

In advising students about their prospects at private schools, Mr. Dix relied heavily on Barron's *Profiles of American Colleges* to help students understand selectivity and find their place in the college hierarchy.

I'll give them copies of this [Barron's]. After we identify an area that they're going to be most comfortable applying to, I'll make some copies of this and they can go back and look through here and see what's realistic.

Mr. Dix keeps a supply of "The Common Application" on hand in the UHS career center to make the process easier for private school applicants. He finds that the private college applicants demand more of his time than public college applicants. Comparing the public and private college applicants, Mr. Dix said:

The only real difference is that if they need that recommendation. . . . most of the students will wind up going to a public university, in spite of all the other stuff that we're talking about. You spend an inordinate amount of time in that respect dealing with private school applications, given where everybody winds up going.

Mr. Dix encourages students to file five to six applications. Often, he finds that UHS students file too many applications.

I got one person applying to thirteen private schools the other day, and they were all in the same sort of general range of Ivy League . . . which I hate to see, because it's a waste of money and it's a waste of places in the school. If they get accepted at six or seven, obviously they're only going to go to one, and so they've tied up a place that somebody else might have been able to get their nose in the door.

Mr. Dix's schema for a more reasonable number of applications is as follows: one to two of the schools students apply to should be reaches, one to two should be good shots, and one school should be a safety. "They usually want to try to get into some school that's probably unrealistic. And I really try to discourage them in that, but they'll do it anyhow." Mr. Dix perceives his role as helping students develop an idea of what was realistic.

> I encourage them, particularly in the junior year . . . to come in and start talking to me about their ideas and showing them some of the college guides, looking at their grades, trying to get an idea of what's realistic and what's not.

Students usually come to Mr. Dix with preconceptions of where they should go. "There are very few who sort of start with a blank slate and start looking through college guides." Mr. Dix sees parents and friends as the dominant influence for UHS students. Parents' own college experiences dominate their visions of what their child should do. They tell them to "apply to the old alma mater, regardless of their qualifications." Even so, Mr. Dix "rarely" attempts to suggest colleges "just because there are so many of them out there. I usually suggest college guides instead."

Mr. Dix sees his role in the college application process as helping students by reading essays and talking about deadlines and "urging them to come in and talk to me." He keeps a file drawer for private school applications yet,

> UC and Cal State I don't pay attention to because they do those applications totally on their own. . . . I'm just keeping track here of the private school applications.

The private college applications demand more of Mr. Dix's attention because they require a school report and recommendation from the guidance counselor. He is not sure how many private school recommendations he writes.

> Probably I guess close to 100 letters of recommendation . . . out of a class of 360. I'm sure by the time I'm through this process it will be probably close to 200.

To be able to write knowledgeably and persuasively Mr. Dix gives students a Career Planning Sheet that asks them their parents' occupation and employer, their favorite subjects, extracurricular activities, awards, and to complete five brief essays about themselves. He also asks the students to have two to three teachers send him comments that he can use in his letter of recommendation.

> Most of the letter, in spite of the fact that I've been following them for four years, the irony of that aspect is that you spend the first two or three years dealing with discipline problems and attendance problems, and the better students you never see till the end of their junior year. So I really rely a lot on that information sheet to write a rec-

ommendation. . . . the better students are just out there being better students, and they're not spending a lot of time with the counselor.

His poignant remarks underscore the limitations of this system for college guidance.

Mr. Dix is supported by Jill Dean, a private counselor in the local community who was hired by the school district as University High School's official College Information Aide. She directs the Career Center, supervises the approximately forty-five parent volunteers, and as Mr. Dix proclaims

does a lot of the college advising around here . . . she provides much the same sort of service here that that type of counselor does on the outside. And that's all she has to really do . . . so she's able to do quite a bit of that with the kids who want to come in.

Mrs. Dean said her position was created by the district a few years ago, in response to a needs assessment done by the parents. The school district determined that this service was needed, thus it was established. Mrs. Dean graduated from Middlebury College, taught elementary school for many years, and occupied this position since it was created.

She keeps detailed records for UHS on where every senior applies, is accepted, and eventually enrolls. She sends these data on applications and enrollments to the district office, which keeps joint records on UHS and other high schools in the district. This information is distributed to students in the *College Application Guide*, which is the school district's booklet for informing students and parents of alumni admissions rates at various colleges. Each University High School alumni, identified only as a grade point average and SAT score, is listed so UHS students can assess their prospects at these same colleges.

Mrs. Dean coordinates the College Visit Program and arranges for many college representatives to visit University High School. Her estimate is that just over 100 colleges send representatives, and up to forty students attend each session. The visits are posted on the calendar outside of the Guidance and Counseling Offices, announced daily, and written up in the Parent-Teacher-Student Association (PTSA) newsletter, which is sent to families of UHS students. Mr. Dix describes the visits as

a steady flow of people. . . . This time of year they come through probably often three or four a day, from different colleges. . . . They've come through here on such a regular basis for such a long time that it's sort of institutionalized . . . They contact her [Mrs. Dean] and she sets up a date for them.

Mrs. Dean meets with each college representative and discusses changes in UHS curriculum or in the college's admissions requirements. She develops the UHS guide that accompanies every application, giving overall school facts and information. She feels that "one important part of my job is the interface between the school and the colleges," which she describes as a public relations function.

Mrs. Dean also meets individually with students, at their initiative, for an entire academic period, fifty minutes. She estimates that she meets with approximately one-third of the senior class, and many more stop by for contact and information. In her meetings with students, she reviews their activities profiles, discusses their interests, and helps them "with certain colleges that are appropriate." She also reads their essays and offers comments.

University High School distributes a planning guide to students and maintains computer software for college searches, which Mr. Dix hopes helps the students "narrow things down considerably." He distributes this guide to students

> just to get them thinking . . . We also have . . . this Peterson college search on an Apple IIE program in there that kids like to come in and play around with.

Mrs. Dean finds that only about 10 percent to 15 percent of UHS's seniors use the computer search program. Likewise, he finds the Peterson's software fairly complicated and basically limited to those students who have the time and computer inclinations to utilize it.

> It's not perfect, though, because it does funny things when you play around with the program. You sometimes wind up getting such a narrow list or you exhaust all the colleges before you ever get to the end of the questions.

These resources can help to further frame the students' range of opportunities, however. Mr. Dix feels the software and the UHS College Application Guide is

> very helpful . . . [you] often don't have to say anything, you just show them who was accepted and who was rejected in the previous classes, and they can sort of make some decisions for themselves.

Using these resources makes the whole college choice process more impersonal. Mr. Dix does not tell any individual student not to apply to a particular college, but rather gives them basic information to judge their options and make their own decisions.

The career center also publishes a list of each graduate's destination, so seniors can talk to an alumnus about what it is like to attend a particular school. This allows students to have a personal connection at a particular college, thus making those colleges more emotionally accessible.

> If they want to go to Pomona then these are a lot of alums . . . graduates over the last three years generally speaking who are still at the college. They can contact them during their winter break or something and talk to them about the school.

Also, the UHS Parent-Teacher-Student Association publishes a monthly newsletter that includes information on college choice,

> talking about who's coming in terms of college representatives . . . information about college choices and what the options are, and test dates, reminding them about SATs, and that sort of thing.

University High School has a plethora of college choice handbooks in the library section of the career center. Mr. Dix recommends *Barron's* to his students for its encyclopedic look at colleges and selectivity. For more specific help in reviewing a college's climate or habitus, Mr. Dix finds

> the Fisk good reading. The *Insider's Guide* is also a good one, the one that's put out by the Yale Press. . . . I spent one summer just reading the whole *Insider's Guide* because I thought it was a fascinating look at college.

The UHS college guidance program is an interesting counseling program setup: Mr. Dix has the knowledge of the students but not the extensive, specific, up-to-date knowledge of colleges. Mrs. Dean actually brings together the knowledge of college and college counseling. As she stated, "I stay put and maintain college contact and work with the counselor."

Mr. Dix does not see UHS teachers as having a very involved role in influencing students' college choices: "I don't think in a really active sense . . . It would be an informal arrangement." Yet Mr. Dix lauds University High School's range of extracurricular activities that are available for students' nonacademic and leadership development.

> There are just two pages full of clubs up there that I could show you. Obviously all of the various competitive sports. There are at least three sports each season for each sex. A lot of time spent in student government here . . . A small but dedicated group keeps getting into this academic decathlon.

Mr. Dix remarked on University High School's climate for going out-of-state to college. A certain percentage of the UHS student population always wants to go out-of-state. "They want to go to Massachusetts or someplace close. . . . It's a coastal mentality around here. It's almost like there's nothing between Massachusetts and California, except maybe . . . Chicago . . . Ohio." Mr. Dix attributes the interest in Ohio to well-known, familiar schools.

Mr. Dix visits with his juniors and recommends that all students take the PSATs.

> Even if they don't think they're planning to go to college, just so they'll have the experience. . . . And then we encourage them to take the SAT in May of their junior year, so they can retake it in the fall of their senior year if they choose to.

He recommends that some students take the ACTs but "it's amazing how ingrained that SAT gets in this area. For some kids, the SAT is the better test, it tests different things . . . Sometimes they'll do better."

Financial aid counseling is definitely a part of Mr. Dix's counseling responsibilities, independent of his senior class counselor role. "That's just something I've been doing for the last two years." Mr. Dix feels that because of the community's affluence, many UHS students do not seek financial aid.

> A relatively small number worry about it. This is, as you know, a fairly affluent community. We do have an evening in January with a speaker in financial aid . . . and advertise scholarships in the daily bulletin and in the PTSA newsletter . . . the SAC application forms are available, and I've got some information on financial aids. The general advice I usually give them of course, if they're really looking for some money, is to fill the SAC form out and see where they stand. A great many people in this community don't quality for anything. So it becomes a frustrating effort for some of them, I think, to go through that whole process.

University High School's college counseling efforts focus on process more than content. Mr. Dix helps students carry out their own college choice processes but does not help them find their way past the quantifiable admissions data to get a "feel" for particular colleges. The UHS counseling program starts early. Mr. Dix was assigned to a ninth-grade class and remained with that class through graduation. He works with students to develop a four-year plan for college preparation.

The UHS counseling efforts, however, are pretty reactive, responding to student or parent demand for specific counseling but not undertaking any special advising or discussion programs. For the most part, University High School's counseling services are educative, in terms of helping students understand the college hierarchy and to find their place in it. These efforts assume students have prior knowledge of colleges. Finally, at University High School, the complete burden of the college choice decision making process is on the student: hand-holding or any other support services that require a substantial counselor's presence is absent.

Mission Cerrito High School

Why Go to a Community College?

1. You wish to attend a college for one to two years which will give you the training needed to enter a vocation.
2. You wish to begin your college training while remaining in your home community.

3. You are not sure of the academic field of study you wish to pursue. You want to explore various subject areas.
4. You want smaller classes and more personal attention than can be given at a large college or university.
5. You plan to complete a four-year college program; however, for financial reasons you plan to remain at home for the first two years.
6. You want to attend a four-year college, but your grades and/or subjects you took in high school do not qualify you for admission without further preparation.

Mission Cerrito High School (MCHS) Senior Guide Book

In 1863, the first public high school was founded in Mission Cerrito. Today, there are two high schools in the Mission Cerrito Unified School District (MCUSD). Mission Cerrito High School has a total enrollment of a little more than 1,800 students, spread across grades nine through twelve. The enrollment at MCHS, however, fluctuated more than at any other schools in this study because of the high mobility within this community. A demographic profile from a senior survey revealed that MCHS was 60 percent white and 40 percent people of color. The latter group consisted primarily of Asians and Hispanics, with 41 percent of the mothers and 36 percent of the fathers being foreign-born. Most of these parents were Vietnamese, Filipino, and Mexican. At least 24 percent of the seniors reported that English was not the main language spoken at home.

According to the College Board's Guide to Secondary Schools, MCHS is a comprehensive high school serving a middle- to lower-middle-class population. About 7 percent of MCHS's college-bound seniors received a Cal Grant B (which indicates low-income status). According to the survey, many of MCHS's students cannot answer questions about their parents' income "because they don't know ... they don't have any idea." However, the senior survey indicates that the majority of MCHS parents (63 percent) do own their own homes.

Although surveyed in their senior year, many MCHS seniors change their expectations throughout that year. The senior survey reports post-high school intentions. Six percent of MCHS seniors expect to go directly into full-time employment, while 4 percent expect to go directly into the military. Of those students who intend to continue their schooling, 5.5 percent intend to go to a trade school, 49 percent to a local community college, 35 percent to a four-year college, and 5 percent have other plans. The reality of MCHS seniors' next steps, however, is quite different from their intentions. Fifteen percent, not 35 percent, end up in four-year colleges, while 55 percent, not 49 percent go to community colleges, and 6 percent enter the armed services.

At least 24 percent of the mothers have a bachelor's degree or higher education, while 33 percent of the fathers hold similar credentials. Although 71 percent of MCHS seniors feel they know which careers they want to pursue, the senior counselor finds that "when I get kids in the office and I talk one-on-one, it doesn't come anywhere near 71 percent."

MCHS is located fourteen miles away from University High School and Paloma in a lower-middle class and working-class neighborhood. The unassuming high school grounds are neat but fairly pedestrian. The Counseling Office is located at the front of the campus in a building connected to the main administration offices. Upon entering the Counseling Office, a visitor sees the receptionist, Mrs. Phillips. This extremely helpful, friendly, middle-aged woman directs the flow of all counseling traffic. The head of the counseling department has a separate, small office to Mrs. Phillips' right, while the remaining three counselors have modest offices along the periphery of Mrs. Phillips' area. Opposite her desk is a sparsely filled bookcase with college guides and other college choice informational materials. Surrounding Mrs. Phillips are a variety of posters, including a college poster, "Finding the Right College"; an alcoholism poster, "How do you know when it's too much?", and a drunk driving poster, "Some learning disabilities develop over night."

The student-to-counselor ratio at MCHS is 400 to 1. The MCHS counseling system is structured so there is one counselor permanently assigned to the senior class, while each of the other three counselors is alphabetically assigned to one-third of the ninth through eleventh graders. Joe Sirotti is the senior counselor at MCHS. He has BA in History and an MA in Pupil Personnel Services from Santa Clara University, which he described as "so close and I was working here, I could just go right to it, and it seemed perfect." Mr. Sirotti was an English teacher for three years, then switched to counseling. He has been the senior counselor for eight years, but has been in general counseling at MCHS a lot longer.

Historically, this configuration for the counseling program at MCHS is a relatively new development. In 1980, the two MCUSD high schools merged and grappled with two distinct guidance programs. The old Mission Cerrito system assigned a counselor to follow a class for four years, while the other school had an alphabetical plan. "You had A through G, no matter what grade, freshmen, sophomore, junior, seniors. And everyone had a segment." When the schools merged, the principal decided to adopt a new, completely different system, which was developed both for the convenience of the counselors, allowing them to "stay current with the newest ideas," and for the protection of underclassmen. Mr. Sirotti felt that in the prior guidance arrangement, seniors got an inordinate level of attention.

> The noisy wheel gets the oil. And that's what happened. The seniors were in here all the time, and the poor little freshmen and sophomores . . . never got attention.

More importantly, under the old system, Mr. Sirotti found himself getting confused or confusing students as he switched between counseling freshman and seniors, "getting them mixed up and I'm giving the wrong info. For me that was a real pain." He also found it cumbersome to familiarize himself every four years with the necessary college information.

> You'd have to sit down and read . . . college entrance and scholarships and adult ed and on and on . . . you really had to reeducate yourself.

Even as the permanent senior counselor, Mr. Sirotti finds it difficult to relearn this material every few years. He reads relevant brochures from colleges or on financial aid "when I have time." He tries to gain mastery over this information to provide better services to his students: "This way I do it year after year, I get to know all the outside information, and I think it's a little better." The trade-off of the Mission Cerrito college counseling program is that counselors' opportunities to master college informational material comes at the expense of developing strong interpersonal relationships with students.

> I never get to know the kids quite as well as I did before. But I do know the material better than I did before. . . . I think that's the most important to do . . . the right facts.

Yet, Mr. Sirotti feels it is important for student advising to remain consistent. "When you have four people doing senior stuff . . . each person could do it a little differently and then the kids are confused."

Mr. Sirotti believes another benefit of having this system is learning more about individual colleges and accumulating feedback from alumni.

> If you do it over and over and over and over, eventually you get to know the schools, know kind of the high points. And kids come back and talk to you and you get the real scoop on some.

Interestingly, Mr. Sirotti suggests that this counseling system provided an antidote to favoritism. He sees this system as more virtuous than the old one, saying now he greets students as fresh faces.

> They all have the same chance to know me and me to know them, and there's no biases or that kind of favoritism because everybody's equal . . . they all get the same kind of services.

Mr. Sirotti believes another benefit to this system is that there is less pressure for counselors than under the old system. The other counselors particularly did not like the paperwork, graduation demands, and "political pressures" that were thrust upon senior students.

> Parents are always looking for scapegoats if their kid doesn't graduate. So it's the school's fault. And so that kind of pressure they don't like to handle.

MCHS seniors have a wide range of counseling needs and, as a result, Mr. Sirotti extends his expertise beyond college choices and admissions information. The other areas where students need help and information include scholarship information and adult education.

Mr. Sirotti is focused on the fact that with a 10 percent dropout rate, accountability at Mission means keeping seniors on track to graduate, not necessarily to continue on to college. The principal's priority is to make Mr. Sirotti accountable. "If a kid doesn't graduate, why didn't he?" Mr. Sirotti's senior counseling efforts actually begin two weeks before the school year school begins.

> They [the students] have the opportunity to come in and change their schedules and look over things . . . I will call some of my worst situation kids and tell them to come in . . . I take care of the emergencies first.

Mr. Sirotti's priority is handling these emergencies, or preventing dropouts. His first counseling task with a new group of seniors is to assess whether or not they are meeting Mission's graduation requirements. "I get a printout of every student . . . I make a list of those that are deficient and what they're deficient in . . . I know which ones I have to get to right away."

For the first three weeks of school, Mr. Sirotti's main task at MCHS is to define who is a senior and, therefore, part of his caseload. A student at MCHS needs 143 accumulated units to become a senior. Initially, Mr. Sirotti's energy is consumed with determining who meets those criteria. Usually he identifies approximately 150 students with less than the required number of units but who still are registering as seniors. He attempts to troubleshoot for those students, "that's how we start the year."

MCHS college counseling efforts actually begin in the junior year with a college fair.

> I have the UCs, state universities, private schools, and community colleges and financial aid . . . I try to get the parents and the kids . . . to get started so that they can use the summer looking at schools and going around, at least know what they have to do, know the requirements.

This school effort is bolstered by the county-wide college fair.

Mr. Sirotti's expectation is that students and parents will visit colleges during the summer between their junior and senior years. Mr. Sirotti never does any follow-up, however, to verify whether Mission students actually do this. He envisions a college choice process where, in the senior year, students focus on filing applications.

> They only have the month of November to apply . . . so they have to know what they want to do early on . . . I follow up with filling out the applications and the workshops.

As senior year begins, Mr. Sirotti is unaware of students who are or are not college-bound. "The college-bound kids I don't know at first. I can guess by looking at the GPA." His first counseling contact with students is in large groups, up to four classes at a time.

> I have a senior orientation . . . I go through a senior guidebook, I go through college information, I go through graduation.

Obviously, students must know what they need for curricular requirements for college, but the school takes a limited role in supplying this knowledge.

> There are large numbers of college prep kids. Now they all think they're going to college and they don't know the requirements, they don't know anything. Many know some, but the majority of them don't. The marginal kid doesn't. The real top-notch kids are going to workshops or college nights and all that kind of stuff.

The top students of MCHS tend to go to "mostly Santa Clara University and UCs." They are a small percentage of the total MCHS student body, and of that group, a small percentage go to out-of-state schools. Rarely do MCHS students go to Stanford University. Mr. Sirotti did not know if ethnic minority students at MCHS have rates of college-going that match the overall student body continuation rates. Instead, he said he could comfortably say that "a good number of Vietnamese have a higher ratio than any of the other minorities."

Mr. Sirotti does not have a lot of time to spend meeting individually with college-bound seniors, although he claims to spend a lot of time with students, especially those who are academically troubled.

> I see a lot of them . . . They're packed in there. They just sign up to see me . . . This time of the year I see green slips . . . deficiency notices . . . just stacks of them, kids having problems.

Mr. Sirotti does, however, spend a good deal of time with MCHS seniors in groups.

> I go into the social studies class once a month with the senior bulletin, and I spend at least fifteen minutes. . . . It's my way of communicating to them in groups, getting out information. I cover anything from stop cutting classes, motivational stuff . . . I cover deadlines and dates and workshops and that kind of stuff. And then I have a list, always a list of scholarships that I have that have come in that month, and how they can apply.

From those large group counseling meetings, he generates sign-ups for workshops, based on students' intentions to attend either a two- or four-year college "and that's usually how I get most of my college prep."

MCHS has limited material resources to make available to students to assist in their college choice processes, however, one resource is the College Explorer software. This software is authored by the College Board and generates for students "a list of colleges." In addition, Mr. Sirotti conducts a limited number of workshops as well as distributes the California State University and University of California applications. He often explains to students "what an application is, how hard it is to apply, what you do when you apply." For those students who plan to go to private schools, he informs them to call or write for applications. He also goes through, step by step, how to fill out an application, emphasizing the importance of being neat.

For all of those students who wish to attend a UC school, Mr. Sirotti arranges for a UC staff person to come to Mission to methodically review the application. He invites staff from San Jose State University to do the same coaching. "So these kids . . . know how to fill out the applications . . . the importance of it." Mr. Sirotti is cognizant of the needs of students who have after-school jobs, thus scheduling for college information sessions is flexible.

> I hold workshops in the morning . . . or one after school on how to
> apply to college . . . to give those kids . . . the ones working after school
> or sports to come in early in the morning.

His expectations are that by the time November comes around, the students are fully engaged in the college choice process and are clear about their choices. He sees his next job as following up with individual conferences for students who need additional help.

> They're welcome to . . . make an appointment, we go through a book,
> we'll talk about advantages and disadvantages of a four-year versus a
> community college.

After the UC and CSU application periods, Mr. Sirotti finds "it's the private schools that kids come in and ask about."

At Mission Cerrito High, only 15 percent of students attend four-year schools. "Out of that, a very low percentage, I'd say maybe three or four, go out of state." The climate at MCHS for four-year colleges is primarily focused on UCs, Santa Clara University, and some California State Universities, mostly West Valley Community College. "It's amazing, but it's been very consistent through the years."

Some students do come to Mr. Sirotti for advice on how to sort through schools once they face multiple acceptances.

> I'd say 10 percent of the kids that get accepted come in. . . . Our kids
> know where they're going to go, and they probably know at the very
> beginning . . . so it isn't a big problem for them.

He finds that the closer students get to the May 1 acceptance deadline, the more anxious they become and the more difficult it is to make the necessary decisions.

Mr. Sirotti often makes specific recommendations about what types of colleges students should attend. Moreover, he is quite open about trying to steer kids away from leaving home, asking them,

> Is that practical? Would you really feel better living down south than you would up here? . . . is it better for you to move away from home? Can you afford it?

Mr. Sirotti does recommend that MCHS students visit the colleges they are interested in attending. Sometimes, but not often, a student's intended major plays a role in choosing a college. "It's my feeling that the major really isn't that important." More than any other factor, Mr. Sirotti comes back to comfort as being the most important reason for college choice: "If they like the atmosphere, they like the school, chances are they will do a whole lot better."

Mr. Sirotti forcefully makes recommendations for those students who apply to a UC and do not get accepted. His advice is "the best bet is to go to the community college not to the state universities." This recommendation is based on two factors: first, he feels ill-prepared to advise students about the large number of CSU campuses, and second, he views the transfer possibilities as being stronger at community colleges.

> If they want to go to the UCs they have a far better chance of being . . . accepted than they do from the state universities. . . . the universities are really obligated to take them. And they do, and they do give them top priority. . . . Now that isn't to say that it's impossible, but it certainly is advantageous to be coming from a community college.

Mr. Sirotti stays current on admissions requirements for California postsecondary institutions by attending professional conferences on articulation between the UC, CSU, and community college systems. He also keeps abreast of the latest transfer potential options.

> The universities tell us there is a high correlation between those coming from . . . the community colleges to the UCs doing very well. So that's why I recommend them to do it.

Students often ask for Mr. Sirotti's advice on the advantages of going to a four-year college, as well as for his educated guess about their admissions eligibility: "Do you think I could make it into San Jose State?" Students also are quite concerned about the stigma of going to a community college.

> Usually it's, "What are the advantages or disadvantages of going to a community college?". . . there's a stereotype among our kids that anyone who goes to a community college is kind of like a second-rate student.

The majority of Mission students who go to college end up going to a two-year institution. Mr. Sirotti sees this as self-selecting.

> The kid who doesn't have the requirements and he reads what he needs and realizes, "Hey, I can't make it to four-year," that's a fact of life, they learn that.

As Mr. Sirotti sees it, for students bound for community colleges "there's not a whole lot of work to do" because he views their fates as sealed by mid-senior year. Instead, the task for those students is to decide among the three local community colleges: DeAnza, West Valley, and Mission. Mr. Sirotti finds himself spending a fair amount of time counseling community college-bound students who "want to know which one would be better for them."

Besides the three community colleges, an occasional MCHS student will attend San Jose City College or Fresno Community College. Yet there are so few students who wish to attend these schools that Mr. Sirotti does not bother to invite representatives from those institutions to come to MCHS to recruit. For interested students, Mr. Sirotti offers the following comparisons of the three community colleges.

> They go to DeAnza because they heard it's the best school around . . . full of collegiate atmosphere, full of activities, things are happening there all the time. Large classes, large selection. They don't like Mission because . . . it's more like a shopping center. It's all indoors . . . very little social or extracurricular activities . . . no football team. It's really a place to go if you want to learn a subject . . . it's so close and really the counseling . . . the teacher ratio's . . . and the teacher involvement with the students is the best at Mission. But the collegiate atmosphere wins, and so that's why they go there [DeAnza]. And to me, I would recommend West Valley over all of them because of its beauty and it's not as large.

Although 60 percent of Mission Cerrito students enter their senior high school year intending to attend a four-year college, that number drops to just 15 percent when they become familiar with the details of the University of California and California State University requirements. It is noteworthy and unfortunate that students only discover these requirements in their senior year, when there is no time to change their curricular course. This change from unrealistic to realistic expectations happens suddenly, "when they see the applications and they start hearing about the requirements . . . that weeds them out."

Interestingly, although many MCHS students are accepted at four-year schools, often they choose not to go. Staying at home and keeping their high school jobs play an important role in deciding where to go to college.

We may get more than 50 percent of the kids accepted to four-year schools, but only about 15 percent will go because of money or because of jobs. They have a job in this area, why leave . . . Jobs play a very important role.

Fifty percent of MCHS student have a part-time job, working ten hours a week or more. Mr. Sirotti feels that after-school jobs often provide "excellent experience" but that they also siphon off important time and energy from academic and college pursuits.

Most MCHS students do not get their information about particular colleges from individual research, although "a very small percentage" did. According to Mr. Sirotti, MCHS students get their information from him, friends, peers, and from their parents' friends and peers. Many students say "Well my next-door neighbor or somebody graduated from there." According to Mr. Sirotti, parents are "the biggest influencing factor other than the student himself," and he notes that a lot of students come to him expressing a parental desire for a particular college, usually an alma mater.

Mr. Sirotti is certain that the well-attended college fair is a valuable consumer information source for MCHS students. That event has over 100 representatives from colleges and universities from across the United States and is sponsored by Santa Clara University.

MCHS freely distributes a senior guidebook, written by Mr. Sirotti, to assist students in selecting their vocational paths and college choices. This guidebook offers minimal suggestions like "organize, develop, and write a concise and informative essay." In this booklet, Mr. Sirotti advises students in their essays to introduce themselves, describe how a college education would benefit "you and your community," discuss curricular, extracurricular, and work experiences, and "write about your personal, education, [sic] and career goals." He also recommends doing rough drafts, editing, and proofreading.

Mr. Sirotti updated and rewrote this eighty-one-page spiral-bound document every year. He had been able to do so because the five-dollar cost of the booklet was made available through school improvement funds. However, since those funds have "dried up," MCHS and Mr. Sirotti now purchases and distributes a college planning guide developed by a neighboring county's Office of Education. (This is the same booklet used by Gate of Heaven counselors.) Because of economies of scale, this booklet's sixty-five-cent cost is impossible to beat, and it saves Mr. Sirotti "a lot of work of updating." He does have some misgivings about the switch because "it's good PR to have your own. . . . The parents think it's great and they really do like the book."

Mr. Sirotti does not keep any records, therefore he does not know the final postsecondary destinations of MCHS students. He feels what is important is to have high graduation rates and a broad understanding of the types of institutions to which MCHS students go.

I never know where they end up because sometimes that changes in the summertime . . . some colleges send us information as to who's been accepted.

Mr. Sirotti faces major limitations in carrying out the work of supporting students' college applications. Although he writes a lot of recommendations, he does not use computer technology or word processing.

I do a lot of letters of recommendation . . . and I do letters on scholarships . . . I do one good one for each student and then I keep it and I mimeograph it off. . . . Places like Stanford and some other schools make it difficult because they ask you specific questions so I may have to do more for them than I would others.

Mr. Sirotti was forthright about the fact that there are no obvious influences that Mission Cerrito High School exerts on students' decision making process. "The school doesn't really go out of its way to recruit or get them to go anywhere. There's no favorite that I know of." He sees MCHS teachers as exerting little influence in students' college choice processes.

There are "a lot of options" for extracurricular activities at MCHS, including sports, clubs, and cheerleading groups. Mr. Sirotti notes that MCHS can, and on occasion does, influence students' college decision making through athletic or other extracurricular activities.

Again, no records are kept, but Mr. Sirotti guesses that Mission Cerrito High students do not file many applications.

Maybe three, and there's excesses on either side. Some guy just goes to one, and some apply to six or seven. It costs forty-five dollars or so to apply for each one, and that's a lot of money, so you're putting out a helluva lot of money just to apply. But we have those that do.

Mr. Sirotti did not know how many students at MCHS took the SATs or ACTs and was apologetic about how constrained his ability to do his job was. He likened himself to a "general practitioner in a sense. I have to handle the whole gamut." The College Board estimated that approximately 45 percent of the MCHS senior class take the SATs.

In summary, Mission Cerrito begins its college counseling program quite late—the senior year. The school, except for an occasional teacher who writes a recommendation and the counseling office, is not very involved in helping students in their college choice decision making process. Mr. Sirotti's basic approach is non-intervention, although for most students he advocates attending a community college immediately after graduation. The college guidance program is reactive and offers minimal, rushed individual appointments to the few students who request time to ask specific college choice questions. Mission Cerrito also suffers from severe resource limitations and has little to offer students in the way of guide-books, publically available software, or support services outside of a single, limited-focus college counseling guidebook. That guidebook also is limited in its emphasis on the community college option, albeit the most prevalent option selected by Mission students. Most important is the competing pressure the MCHS counseling staff faces, often resulting in limited counseling time being devoted to dropout prevention than to college guidance.

CHAPTER FOUR

A Cross-Case Analysis
of High School Guidance

This cross-case analysis of the college counseling programs at Paloma, Gate of Heaven, University, and Mission Cerrito high schools is not an assessment of each individual counselor's effectiveness or biases. It focuses on understanding how each high school's different structural arrangements affect the operation of the college advising processes occurring within them and is an analytic and evaluative description of each school's college counseling efforts that examines:

- the goals and objectives underpinning the college guidance program,
- the total resources devoted to college preparation and how college advising efforts are structured, and
- the impact for students' perceptions of their college opportunities and the actual outcomes.

This chapter also examines how the structuring of college guidance in high schools follows class-based patterns, exhibiting important similarities across high schools serving students with similar class backgrounds.

This chapter shows that individual guidance counselors have a direct impact on students, and more importantly, that the counselor is critical in constructing the school's expectations and formal planning for college. The counselor creates and implements the school's organizational response to college planning and, as such, creates an organizational worldview that serves to delimit the full universe of possible college choices into a smaller range of manageable considerations. The school and the counselor construct this worldview in response to their perceptions of the parents' and community's expectations for appropriate college destinations, combined with their own knowledge and experience base. I view each school as the mediator of the collective social class consciousness of the community that it serves.

89

Prior studies document little or no positive impact of guidance counselors on students (Hotchkiss and Vetter 1987). Yet, daily, students and counselors in these schools experience physical and organizational conditions that influence the frequency and nature of interactions surrounding college planning. Students and counselors at each school interpret their needs differently from the needs of students and counselors at the other three schools and have widely differing ideas about their social class communities. These are local understandings about what it means to go to college and which colleges are appropriate.

What shapes the quality of everyday school experiences and interactions is a school's context: policies, resources, and organizational structures. Jeannie Oakes (1989) has demonstrated the value of assessing a school's context; information about context supplements the more commonplace quantitative assessments of student outcomes and offers insights into why particular student outcomes are enabled or constrained. For example, documenting the school context points out whether and how high school students are encouraged to aspire in terms of college goals. Or, detailing the school context can highlight a school's problem areas and strengths that operate most effectively as the mediators between school, community, family resources, and student outcomes. Moreover, a careful examination of the school context illuminates organizational arrangements and policies and emphasizes a school's decisions about how and why school resources are allocated as they are.

The guidance office is one of two units of analysis in this book but it is the singular focus of this chapter. The other unit of anlysis is the family, and its impact will be discussed in the next chapter. To understand an individual's perceptions of the opportunities that are available this analysis looks at the high school and, later, in Chapter Five, examines the individual's family, peers, and geographical and social communities.

March and Simon (1958) note that the basic features of organizational structure stem from universal problem-solving needs: because of limited intellectual capacities, people cannot make decisions that involve major cognitive complexity. People require simplified models that capture only the main features of a problem. Moreover, because of time and resource limitations, most decision making is based on a search for satisfactory alternatives. These constraints are necessary because optimizing decision making requires extremely complex processes.

When choosing a college, a student's decision-making process is affected by both the normative expectations that exist among the students, parents, and faculty of a high school, as well as by anticipated consequences and what alternatives will be considered or ignored. Specifically, a student's perceptions of available alternatives are conditioned by her social status and the environmental evoking mechanism—the guidance process. This combination of social networks and environment is an individual's frame of reference for college planning. If the frame of reference and perceptions are congruent, as in the case of an upper middle-class student seeking to attend a "good" college, then there is no dissonance. But, if in trying to choose a college, a student has a frame of reference that conflicts with her perceptions about what is available to her, she will filter out choices that are too discordant (March and Simon 1958). An example would be an academically talented student from a low-SES background or school who refuses to consider a University of California because she does not feel she would be comfortable there.

The critically important question in evaluating the high school's role in facilitating the transition to college is: What impact does the high school, and, specifically, the guidance counselor, have on enabling or constraining students in securing adequate college preparation and the necessary information about college choice? More importantly, if the school's college counselors do not take into account important status characteristics such as available cultural capital, then the counseling services will differentially impact students from different social classes (McDonough 1988).

The guidance process impacts students through subtle and unobtrusive controls. This process assumes that students are familiar with the communication channels for the transmission of college information, know the specialized college choice vocabularies, and are aware of the necessary deadlines and appropriate timetables. High schools influence individual students by how they structure the flow and content of information, make explicit expectations that highlight or downplay specific options, limit the search for alternatives, and impose a specific schedule (Perrow 1979). Another important influence is the assumption the school makes about how familiar students are with basic information and prerequisites. Whatever college choice assistance the guidance office offers enhances or detracts from students' cultural capital.

The guidance counselor is the organizational representative who summarizes her or his own perceptions and transmits them to the rest of the school, thus becomes an important source of information within the high school. Bounded rationality frames the analysis of school habitus by looking at the ways in which each high school helps seniors limit their search for college choices to a manageable number of considerations. These high schools suggest appropriate choices to students, highlight certain goals for college, assume a status background regarding the majority of students, arrange the physical layout of the guidance operation, and provide environmental stimuli.

Overview Guidance Structure and Outcomes

Table 4.1 offers some basic information about the four schools in this study and how they have constructed a college guidance program to assist college-bound seniors. Paloma's counselor to student ratio of 1:56 is comparable to the U. S. private preparatory school average of 1:65 (Cookson and Persell 1985). Gate of Heaven's ratio of 1:117 is lower than the 1:235 U. S. average for Catholic schools

TABLE 4.1
Organizational Comparisons

	Paloma School	*Gate of Heaven High School*	*University High School*	*Mission Cerrito High School*
Students	210	450	1280	1800
Seniors	56	117	365	400
Counselors	1	1	1	1
Time on Guidance (%)	100	100	90	50
Average Time Per Student	10–15 hrs.	1 hour	45 min.	—

(Coleman, Hoffer, and Kilgore 1982). Although the nationwide average for public schools is 1:323, California's statewide estimate is one counselor per 848 students. University High School's ratio of 1:365 is better than both the United States and California averages, while Mission Cerrito's average of 1:400 is better than the California average.

How much of each counselor's effort is devoted to college planning ranges from 50 percent of Mr. Sirotti's total counseling effort to 100 percent of Mrs. Ball's effort at Paloma. The time each counselor spends with every senior is just as striking, ranging from no estimate per individual for Mr. Sirotti to ten to fifteen hours per student for Mrs. Ball. Although Ms. Trent's estimate is only one hour, she does spend considerable time with students individually and in groups throughout their high school years at Gate of Heaven. What follows is a summary of each school's college counseling program.

College curricular and counseling functions are the centerpiece of Paloma's raison d'etre—college preparation—the very essence of being at Paloma, as such, evident to one degree or another in almost every student-staff interaction. Moreover, all of Mrs. Ball's efforts and all course content are directed at preparing Paloma students for college. Mrs. Ball spends a lot of time meeting with students one-on-one. She advises and supports them in developing specific plans, including a dream school, a small number of reasonable choices for colleges, and at least one safe admissions bet. Mrs. Ball is acutely aware of the admissions environment and attempts to help students manage their application process, acceptances, and rejections. Assuming that all students intend to pursue college and are familiar with the types and ranges of colleges, Paloma counselors do not begin explicit counseling for specific college choices until midway through the junior year. However, the staff does not leave a student's curricular preparation to chance: all courses are tailored to offer students maximum college choices without unnecessarily narrowing the range of curricular offerings.

Gate of Heaven staff assumes that students know little about college types or requirements and have developed a detailed four-year effort to prepare the young women. Ms. Trent provides students with increasingly more complex information on options over their four years of high school. Gate of Heaven's college counseling efforts include individualized counseling, group discussions, and teacher involvement, as well as the provision of books and technology for additional support. The college counseling program assumes that students need basic information about college planning, as well as nurturance and support. College guidance at Gate of Heaven begins immediately in the ninth grade and continues throughout the student's high school career.

University High School faces a reality of numbers: the college counselor cannot effectively advise all of the 365 seniors, let alone guide the efforts of every college-bound student. Consequently, the counseling program focuses on helping students set up a four-year curricular plan that meets prerequisites for admissions to most four-year colleges. Then the college counselor informs groups of students how to comply generically with admissions norms. Mr. Dix primarily helps students with the University of California and California State University systems' processes; he does not try to assist students with the quagmire of specific climate or the feel of individual campuses, public or private. University High School's college counseling efforts historically have been subject to influence by parental or student demand. The most notable example of this was establishing a college advising center and hiring an aide (Mrs. Dean) to staff an office that would provide more individual attention to at least some subpopulation of students. University High School's counselors assume a fixed hierarchy of college opportunities and attempt to help students find their place in that hierarchy, based on an immutable combination of GPA and SAT scores. There is no assumption that students may be able to manipulate those numbers or that many private colleges might offer better opportunities. Students at University High School bear the onus of responsibility for college choice decision making: Mr. Dix is unable to provide time for intensive individual counseling or for shepherding through the emotions of the admissions process.

Mission Cerrito, of all of the high schools in this study, begins its college counseling program the latest. Students are not seen or even addressed in groups regarding college options until their senior year. The counselor, Mr. Sirotti, is a non-interventionist in individual college decision making. His competing organizational demands nearly preclude his seeing students individually, and he has little or no time to keep up on specific entrance requirements or on information about different curricula available. Almost across the board, Mr. Sirotti advocates attending one of the three local community colleges immediately after graduation. He does this in groups, written materials, and the rare one-on-one situation. The MCHS college guidance program is reactive, offering minimal information on UC and CSU schools. What little is offered is often delivered by professionals from those nearby campuses most frequently attended by MCHS students. Mission

TABLE 4.2
College Continuation Rates

	Paloma School	Gate of Heaven High School	University High School	Mission Cerrito High School
To College (%)	98	91	89	70
To Two-Year College (%)	2	32	18	55
To Four-Year College (%)	96	59	71	15
To Private College (%)	55	15	31	★
To UC (%)	36	11	39	★
To CSU (%)	0	33	11	★

★Not available.

Cerrito suffers from severe resource limitations, with little to offer students in the way of college guidebooks or commercially available software. MCHS's commitment to college preparation is minimal outside of the counseling office, although some teachers write letters of recommendation or answer a student's occasional question about college.

What do these different high school contexts enable or constrain in terms of students' college planning? The first indicator of the influence of these diverse school contexts is in students' college destinations. Table 4.2 shows which students go on to which type of colleges at the four schools. In terms of baseline college continuation, Paloma sends almost all of its students to college, Gate of Heaven and University High School send approximately nine out of ten students, and a little over half of Mission Cerrito's students go directly on to college. However, the aggregate data do not tell the whole story. The types of colleges these students attend vary quite a bit.

Nearly all Paloma students go to either a University of California or a private four-year school, while just over half of Gate of Heaven girls go to four-year schools. The remaining Gate of Heaven students, 32 percent, go to community colleges. The 59 percent of Gate of Heaven's college-bound students who go to four-year colleges attend a more heterogeneous mix of schools than do Paloma students: 33 percent go to California State Universities, 15 percent to private schools, and only 11 percent to UC schools. Approximately two-thirds of the 11 percent of Gate of Heaven students who are enrolled at University of California campuses are within fifteen to fifty miles of their homes.

Meanwhile, University High School students resemble their high-SES Paloma counterparts insofar as two-thirds of these students go to four-year schools. Unlike Gate of Heaven girls, they are more evenly distributed between

UCs (39 percent) and private (31 percent) colleges, with only 11 percent at CSU campuses. Mission Cerrito students follow totally different college pathways: 55 percent of them go directly to one of the three junior colleges in their community. Of those students at four-year schools, it is impossible to say how students are distributed among private, University of California, and CSU schools because Mission Cerrito keeps no records of students' destinations. However, Mr. Sirotti did indicate that a small number of students go to Santa Clara University and a significant portion of students bound for four-year schools end up at San Jose State University. A handful of students, the superstars at MCHS, go on to University of California campuses or occasionally to prestigious private colleges.

With this overview of the guidance structure and outcomes for each of the high schools, it is important to understand several pieces of the structure in greater depth in order to lay the foundation for how an organizational structure becomes an organizational habitus. A leading organizational analyst describes how every structure has a normative component, which includes its values, norms, and role expectations (Scott 1992). Thus, each high school presented has values related to college continuation that are embodied in its organizational mission and curriculum, norms that are built into what assumptions it makes about students' prior college knowledge and expectations of how college counselors will enact their roles. The next section will highlight each school's mission and curriculum, the assumptions of students, and counselors' roles.

Organizational Mission and Curriculm

The high school guidance office provides a social context that influences individual behavior. This office's structure is a symbolic medium that guides student's thinking about the college decision-making process. As we have seen, Paloma's and Gate of Heaven's college counseling efforts are fully dedicated to college continuation, as are nine out of ten guidance hours at University High School. Everything about these schools' guidance operations conveys the expectation that most, if not all, students should continue on to college and, if possible, good colleges. This message is evident from Mrs. Ball's individual meetings to the constant group discussions at Gate of Heaven to the four-year plans developed between Mr. Dix and UHS students. Mission Cerrito is in a category of its own: at most, 50 percent of Mr. Sirotti's effort is devoted to assisting students who are college-bound, or approximately 65 percent of seniors.

The professional services offered by these guidance offices also provide an organizational mechanism for the mutual pursuit of individual and organizational goals. Paloma and University high schools each keep detailed records of graduates' destinations. They use these records both to offer parents evidence that their schools help students reach appropriate college destinations and as networking and insider information for guiding students who may be interested in following in their predecessors' footsteps at particular colleges. Gate of Heaven keeps aggregate records of destinations but does not organize an effort to link alumnae with students who are interested in particular schools. Mission Cerrito does not even keep records of post-high school destinations.

Institutional sagas or cultures develop over time (Clark 1970) and are important because they represent the articulated and formalized values of the institution. Each of the four high schools in this study has historically valued college continuation differently. Paloma is a college preparatory school committed to the highest standards, while University High School claims it has a "national reputation for academic excellence. . . . and a strong belief in quality public education." Gate of Heaven has always had a mission to educate women to serve their communities and families and has been sending a good number of young Catholic women to college for some time. Mission Cerrito is a comprehensive high school for a middle- to a lower-middle class population for which attending college is not so much facilitated as expected, primarily in the community college tradition (*Guide to Secondary Schools* 1986).

Preparatory schools are the standard bearers of maximal college planning. The number-one mission of a college preparatory school is to enable students to get into the "best" colleges possible. Paloma devotes considerable resources to this mission. In addition to a dedicated college preparatory curriculum, these schools generally provide extensive individual counseling and detailed written guidelines for students and families about the college decision-making process. Moreover, counselors are in close contact with selective college admissions personnel and engage in and refine the art of writing letters of recommendation (Cookson and Persell 1985). Mrs. Ball does all of these things, while her counterparts at the other three schools do only some of them, to varying extents.

College destinations are strategic responses to a decision-making process involving two major components: academic preparation (college readiness) and admissions planning and execution (college choice). According to one estimate, 75 percent of American 18-year-olds have not taken a strong academic curriculum, therefore do not have the curricular prerequisites for a four-year liberal arts college (Cookson and Persell 1985). Although most U. S. high schools have both a vocational and college preparatory curriculum, the balance of organizational resources devoted to curricula depends on the historical character of the student population and its eventual destinations.

All of Paloma's students take the necessary curricula to minimally meet the admissions requirements for four-year colleges. Counselors at both UHS and Gate of Heaven try to supply information to students early on to help them develop a four-year course plan that will ensure their preparation for application to four-year colleges. Cindy Lane, a student at University High School, describes her curricular preparation.

> You kind of guess at what you're going to take. . . . through your se-
> nior year. The four-year plan. And those aren't the classes you're nec-
> essarily going to take; it's just an outline of the classes you're going to
> take, and the requirements, and the classes that count for UC credit,
> or the classes that count for State, and whatever.

All of the students at Gate of Heaven, Paloma, and University high schools spoke
positively about their school's curricular advisement services. Those students met
the challenge head on and took the requisite courses. Constance Evans found that
UHS's course graduation requirements match "the requirements you need to get
into most colleges, like state, UC, or you know, private colleges," and although she
would not have voluntarily chosen them first, she is glad she took them.

Mission Cerrito students voiced many complaints about inadequate counseling attention and problems resulting from being placed in inappropriate courses. Because of the way Mission Cerrito has designed its advisement program, counselors
assigned to freshmen, sophomores, and juniors are not familiar with college admissions processes, yet they advise students on their yearly course choices. They, like Mr.
Sirotti, are faced with high caseloads (400 students per counselor) and more specifically, are called upon to deal with the whole panorama of student counseling needs:
discipline, dropout prevention, and personal and family problems. Samantha, Carol,
and Kay particularly felt that the MCHS college counseling system was poor.

In junior high, Samantha had circled a response on a form indicating that
she was planning to go to college. In eighth, ninth, and tenth grades her counselor
came into one of her classes and handed out information sheets about the University of California and CSU admissions requirements.

> I was just pretty much working for State (CSU) requirements. Well it
> said biology, and well I had human biology . . . I was just signing up
> for what I thought I needed to have. You turn it in and they sign you
> up for those classes.

With counselor approval, Samantha signed up for two years of science, one
of which was a human biology course. In her junior year, she discovered her two
years of science would suffice for graduation requirements but that human biology was not enough biology to meet the CSU requirements. At that point, she
made an appointment to see her counselor. The counselor "didn't even realize I
was college" bound, which was difficult for Samantha. "The counselor obviously
just overlooked it or didn't think . . . I don't know what happened." Because a lot
of MCHS advising happens via group sessions or paperwork, problems often are
identified too late because "they just talked to everybody in the whole class at
once. It wasn't like individual." So, as a senior, Samantha had to take biology again,
this time the CSU prerequisite course, surrounded by sophomores with whom she
felt out of place. She hated the whole experience.

Carol Lincoln also suffered from inadequate advising. She labeled herself as arriving at MCHS "messed up" because her junior high school counselor had inappropriately informed her about which biology course to take. "That was another reason why I was thinking about going to junior college." As was the case with her entire college choice process, Carol, without the help or encouragement of her MCHS counselor, decided to apply to a CSU school and was conditionally accepted: "I have to take biology when I first get there."

Kay knew she had no other choice but a community college option, because her grades foreclosed anything else.

> I have to go to junior college before I can go to college. There's no way I can get into any college right now. . . . see I never took college preparatory classes. I mean I started out and they were just too hard so I gave up and just went to the easier stuff.

Like most MCHS students, Kay does not consider junior college a real college, but it seemed relatively hassle-free.

An organization's communication system will be most burdened when it is concerned with the less-structured aspects of its tasks, particularly when explaining problems that are not well-defined. For the student who is first in her family to go to college, the tasks of preparing and planning for college will be less well-defined than for the individual who has generations of college-going relatives. The students who fared somewhat better at Mission Cerrito were Edie, Julie, and Lucy. These three girls had two things in common: first, all felt that they received good junior high counseling for their high school classes, and second, they all had parents who had gone to four-year colleges and were involved early on with their daughters' college planning. As Kanter (1977) notes, a basic feature of organizational life is a structure of opportunity, which affects the individual's perception of mobility. Opportunity is dynamic and relates a participant's present position to their potential mobility. For high school students bound for college, placement in the college track is the baseline measure of their opportunities. Students with cultural capital are advantaged by having family members who can explain that there are high-mobility paths within the college track. Edie Tashimi was placed into the highest-tracked math, science, and English courses at MCHS. From junior high school on, Edie was placed in advanced classes: "They just recommend you to be in certain classes . . . I guess you're just put in there. I don't really know how they do that."

Both Julie and Lucy, however, had mixed experiences with Mission Cerrito. Their junior high counselor helped them set up their high school courses. As Lucy put it, "They just give you your classes . . . College just seemed so far away, I didn't even think about it." Although both sets of parents helped their daughters plan their courses, they were not really familiar with the hierarchically tracked nature of the college preparatory courses at MCHS, which offered college preparatory classes in the general or advanced varieties. Lucy, who was "in mostly general" courses, was keenly aware that the tracked nature of courses was set early on and "always tend to be the same people, like they are ever since elementary school."

Subsequent course advising happened, as Lucy described it, when the counselor came into a class to discuss general college requirements, such as "what you need to get into a college—a four-year, or J.C., or university." However, when senior year began, Lucy had the feeling that her college choice process had "just snuck up on me." As she sorted through the choices, applying and figuring out what she wanted, she felt "kind of like in shock . . . I have to plan my life right now, I don't know what I want to do." She consulted with her counselor, her parents, and looked at the MCHS Senior Guide Book, grappling with "if I wanted to go away or stay around here. I still don't know what I want to do."

In spite of Lucy's feeling of floundering, Mrs. Baker had a positive view of the high school's role in Lucy's college planning. She recalled that the school had mailed information during Lucy's freshman year regarding the required high school courses. "The high school was very, very good . . . has just been a really major part of helping the family to know what direction to take."

Disgruntled with MCHS for other reasons, Julie felt the school and counselor played a role in lowering her expectations to attend a community college, even though her parents encouraged her to go to a four-year school. Julie felt discouraged by Mr. Sirotti, not in a face-to-face meeting where he assessed her credentials and opportunities, but through his group presentations. Although Mr. Sirotti spoke in general terms, the impact was significant for her as an individual.

> Mr. Sirotti said that was probably the best thing. Not just me, but for anybody in general in my class, it's the best way to get used to . . . he generalizes . . . when he told us about the junior college . . . he didn't say it as a form of being kind of a cop-out, he said it in a form of being an excellent idea if you didn't want to go right away into a four-year college.

During her senior year, Julie did see Mr. Sirotti in a personal interview "before the first quarter ended," which was after she had submitted her four-year college applications. After she informed him about her choices he said, "a really good way to do it is to go two-year and transfer to a four-year."

Julie, however, was quite concerned that the junior colleges in the area did not have a good reputation. Although she did not perceive a pressure at MCHS to attend four-year colleges, she did notice that "you get a good pat on the back if you say you're going . . . to a university, they go, 'Wow,' you know, 'how exciting.'" In the final analysis, both Lucy and Julie felt inadequately prepared for college, finally opting to "brush up" at the local community colleges.

Assumptions of Students' College Knowledge

As presented here, Paloma and University high schools each assume family knowledge of college hierarchies. They base their college counseling programs on this knowledge as well as on a certain "taste" (Bourdieu 1984) for colleges that are ranked more highly. Gate of Heaven and Mission Cerrito high schools make no such assumptions of prior knowledge, yet the differences in resources and outlook on their organizational missions means that Gate of Heaven has constructed a plan to fill in the knowledge gap, while Mission Cerrito has no time to do so, nor does Mr. Sirotti or the MCHS leadership see it as part of the organizational mission.

However, the high schools' assumptions that all students will be able to rely on families to supplement school information leaves a lot to chance for those students whose parents have not gone to college or whose parents are relatively uninvolved in their children's choices. A first-generation college-bound senior is operating in what for her is uncharted waters and is facing a high degree of uncertainty, both in what college choices to make and how to make appropriate ones. The level of influence any counseling operation has on an individual's behavior is related to the degree of uncertainty it helps the individual absorb.

As we have seen, Mission Cerrito does not have the resources to absorb uncertainty. In fact, Mr. Sirotti's advice that students take the community college route seemingly affected both Julie and Lucy in adding to their uncertainty, highlighting the fact that their high school preparations were not adequate. Both students and their parents eventually acted in ways consistent with these assessments and came to see the community college option as a more suitable first college step. Also, Samantha, who initially was adamant about not going to a community college, eventually capitulated to her mother's and Mr. Sirotti's strong preference. Although she finally agreed to attend the local junior college, the emotional adjustment was hard because she was an integral part of a close circle of nine friends, and everyone else in the group went to a four-year college. She found watching them go through the application processes and waiting periods "depressing because I wanted to go so much, but . . . I'll get there."

Gate of Heaven, aware of the uncertainties of college-going for mostly first-generation students, constructed a four-year college counseling program to help students become emotionally accustomed to the notion of college attendance, moving away from home, and separating from friends. In spite of that effort, only approximately one-fifth of Gate of Heaven students went away to college.

All Paloma students easily filled in the advising gap with family knowledge and sometimes with private counselors, as will be described in Chapter Five. Sometimes the overall climate of expectations of the school will make up for the gap in individual families' knowledge, but this is not a systematic, organizational response to ensure every student's preparation. Individuals who lack college-choice cultural capital are dependent upon the sponsorship of the guidance coun-

selor to help them receive insider information and marshall the organizational resources that back their college applications, since they do not have outside sponsorship. In the case of University High School, this stewardship proved to be
particularly important.

Beginning in her freshman year, Constance Evans often found herself dependent on her friends or on the advice of her counselor for developing her college plans. It was when Mr. Dix met with her to develop a four-year plan that she
first started thinking about college: "Well, I haven't thought about college. I don't
know if I want to do that or whatnot." She did not know what the SATs were
until her counselor "came into our classes" and informed students that the SATs
were coming up. Through her inquiries, she "found out what they were" and discovered that the SATs were required for admission to colleges. In her junior year,
as Constance's friends started talking about their college choices, she began to
think about her own plans. Even then, her basic lack of knowledge about college
planning surprised even her. It was not until she returned from her visit to a
Southern California campus that she realized one school she visited was a private
college. "Actually, I didn't even know that was a private college when I first went
down there."

Constance was quite serious and persistent in her pursuit of receiving assistance from UHS during her college search. She frequently visited with either Mr.
Dix or Mrs. Dean, sometimes consulting with the counselors "three times a week"
on a range of items, from when to submit transcripts to CSU schools to how to
complete financial aid forms. Individuals make competing claims on an organization's resources, and students like Constance, without the cultural capital relevant
to college choice, make more exacting claims. A guidance office not aware of and
responsive to the needs of both high- and low-SES students will offer students different levels of access to their services. University High School appears to be responsive to students if they, like Constance, vigilantly ask for assistance and know
what to ask for and about. If a student who has a class background similar to Constance's did not have friends who kept her informed and on schedule, then the
UHS counseling operation would have no means of stopping the student from
falling through the cracks of its counseling system.

Counselor Role Expectations

It is possible to discern what each high school expects of its college counselors by
looking at how the counselors enact their jobs. Three indicators of this include
looking at counselors' professional networks, the way in which counselors view
the task of writing letters of recommendation for college applicants, and the college advising material resources that are made available to students and parents to
supplement personal counseling.

Professional networks are an important source of information. The types of affiliations and identifications individuals have and act upon offer insight into the person's perceptions of his or her appropriate professional worlds. Preparatory school counselors maintain contact with admissions officers through professional networks, ensuring the careful articulation between their schools and the postsecondary institutions where most of their graduates attend.

Mrs. Ball of Paloma is an active member and attends the annual meetings of the National Association of College Admissions Counselors. Through this professional association, each year, she puts herself in close contact with the admissions officers who will be making decisions about her students. This contact is accomplished in a professional development mode, outside of the institutional setting. This kind of networking and interaction provides Mrs. Ball with insight into what kinds of students fare well at particular institutions and which institutions, in any given year, are looking for particular student characteristics.

Ms. Trent has her own outside consulting business and is connected with other private counselors. She contacts private and public college representatives to visit Gate of Heaven to advise students about opportunities available on their college campuses. Also, Ms. Trent took an unpaid leave of absence from Gate of Heaven to do a recruitment and admissions internship with a local community college during the 1987–88 academic year.

Mr. Dix did not identify any meaningful professional connections other than the college representatives who came through University High School, and even those visits and connections were cultivated and maintained by Mrs. Dean, who works diligently to maintain contact with counselors at particular colleges where UHS graduates frequented. Mrs. Dean also has contact with other private counselors.

Mr. Sirotti is grateful for the professional connections he has with UC and CSU professionals who come to the MCHS campus to inform students about admissions and financial aid procedures for their institutions. He speaks positively about attending local workshops that are sponsored by the state universities for high school counselors. He views the workshops as being a good source of information and insight into admissions prospects at those schools. In summary, Ms. Trent, Mrs. Dean, and Mrs. Ball actively sought contacts and continuing associations with a broad range of public and private college admissions counselors, while Mr. Dix and Mr. Sirotti focused on the UC and CSU networks and standard seminar formats for updating counselors on admissions information.

Letters of recommendation highlight an area where organizational competence and resources are critical. For the most competitive colleges, admissions processes favor candidates whose school personnel write detailed letters of recommendation. Preparatory schools, or any school with highly organized and adequate support for letter writing and other support services, increase their students' admissions options and chances.

Mrs. Ball collects information from classroom teachers to write multi-page letters of recommendation that provide admissions officers with in-depth views of Paloma students. Above and beyond the call of duty, she works on letters for every Paloma senior during summer vacation. Moreover, she was an admissions officer for thirteen years at a competitive Eastern state university and knows what kinds of information and what level of detail is useful to admissions readers.

Mr. Dix also is aware of the need that UHS students have good letters of recommendation. He prepares approximately 200 original letters of recommendation and estimates that he processes 600 to 700 private school applications. He has set aside one of his UHS file drawers to keep track of private school applications and the letters of recommendation he writes for those applicants. He stays current with his letter-writing needs by keeping a wall chart of the entire senior class with an "X" next to each student's name for whom he has already written a recommendation. Mr. Dix's actual familiarity with students is limited, and before senior year he often sees only those students who are in trouble. To aid him in writing the letters of recommendation, he supplies students with an information sheet and asks two to three teachers for their comments so he can become acquainted with the students' academic proficiencies, as well as with their research and extracurricular interests. Because recommendation letters are not required by California public universities and because 50 percent of graduating seniors from UHS go to University of California and CSU campuses, Mr. Dix felt private school applications required "an inordinate amount of time." He admitted that with the UCs and CSUs "it's an easier process for me to deal with" and that he did not pay attention to those applications unless called upon to do so by students.

Both Ms. Trent of Gate of Heaven and Mr. Sirotti of Mission Cerrito respond to students' requests for letters of recommendation but spoke of no particular burdens placed on the counseling systems by the large number of letters that needed to be written, nor did they speak of efforts to write or refine in-depth letters about individual students.

Finally, a common organizational response to helping participants handle large quantities of information and complex tasks is to develop a handbook or practice manual. Paloma, Gate of Heaven, and Mission Cerrito each distribute handbooks to assist students in their college choice processes. Although University High School distributes resource materials to students, there is no overview or "how-to" guidebook developed or distributed by the school.

Mrs. Ball distributes a college handbook to all Paloma students in their junior year. Her explicit purpose is to reach parents regarding two subjects: not to pressure their daughters to aim for out-of-reach colleges and to speak to their daughters about how the family's financial condition may affect final college choices. Paloma's guidebook is designed to fine-tune the efforts of a knowledgeable family, resulting not only in a highly organized and efficient college application process, but also in a rational and sensitive college planning process. In addition, Mrs. Ball advises students on the time management aspect of college choice. Timetables specify what students should be thinking about and doing in each high school year to enhance their chances of getting into the "right" schools.

Ms. Trent distributes not only a college counseling booklet, developed by another source, to Gate of Heaven students, but has over fifteen handouts and free advising materials that she distributes to each student throughout her high school career, mostly in the junior and senior years. Ms. Trent introduced a "College/Career Planning Achievement Award" booklet for juniors and seniors. If students completed at least eight out of ten of the listed steps (for example, visit with a college representative or visit a college campus), they received an achievement award. Also introduced by Ms. Trent were annual checklists for juniors and seniors, which students consulted to stay on track for deadlines. Moreover, both the Career Center's resources and college search software supplemented Ms. Trent's distributed materials.

To initiate University High School students in the college search process, Mr. Dix photocopies pages from Barron's *Profiles of American Colleges* and recommends that students consult Fiske's *Guide to Selective Colleges*.

At MCHS, Mr. Sirotti's college planning guidebook for seniors is an effective vehicle for parents to help their children find a way through the college maze. Some parents praise the MCHS handbook as an example of how Mr. Sirotti's effort enabled them to become partners with their daughters in the college planning process. Mrs. Baker was particularly thankful.

> This year specifically they put out a booklet for the seniors about everything that's going to happen during the year and everything. . . .
> It gave a real good perspective to the seniors.

She also was pleased with the college night meeting Mr. Sirotti arranged for parents to "find out about the junior colleges, about the state program, and the universities." Mrs. Baker felt that MCHS helped with applications, deadlines, and counselor availability. "They gave us basic ideas of when things needed to be taken care of . . . they gave a lot of help at school in terms of filling out applications."

Paloma, Gate of Heaven, and University high schools each had extensive information centers in locations that provided easy and open access for students. MCHS had no such facilities. The handful of available books and computer software and hardware was located in Mr. Sirotti's personal office and obviously was not accessible to individual students to use or to explore.

Summary of Actual and Normative Structure of College Advising

What can we now say about the way in which counselors construct a school context for college choice, and what do each of these schools expect of college-bound students? Table 4.3 summarizes each school's college counseling program. Both

TABLE 4.3
College Counseling Summary

	Paloma School	Gate of Heaven High School	University High School	Mission Cerrito High School
Counseling Begins	eleventh grade	ninth grade	ninth grade	twelfth grade
Support Services	Yes	Yes	No	No
Competing Missions	No	Yes	Yes	Yes
Limited Resources	No	No	Some	Yes

private schools are proactive in their approach to college counseling, dedicate more counseling resources than do their public counterparts, and provide nurturing and supportive services to students, while being specially cognizant of the emotional turmoil involved in the college choice. Both public schools are reactive in providing college counseling, have extremely limited and overtaxed resources, and have little or no time for any additional support services related to college planning.

Counseling begins at each school in uniquely different ways. All Paloma curricular options are designed as college preparatory, assuming that students possess basic familiarity with and have family knowledge of college, while specific college counseling begins in the junior year of high school. Mission, facing limited resources and a burgeoning counselor caseload, begins college counseling in the senior year. Both Gate of Heaven and University high schools begin their counseling efforts in the freshman year. For UHS, the four-year plan is developed and set into motion to ensure curricular readiness, while Gate of Heaven's approach includes not only a four-year plan but slowly introduces students to college types and terms. More importantly, Gate of Heaven begins their students' emotional adjustment by having them picture themselves at college.

Each of these four schools makes different assumptions. Paloma leaves little to chance in the way of curricular preparation, offering students a plethora of advanced placement classes within a curriculum designed to guarantee entry into a four-year college. Paloma's college choice counseling begins in the junior year, assuming that students need assistance from the school in the college choice process but not in basic orientation to college types and options. At Paloma, there are clear-cut and uniform expectations: virtually all of the students will go to college, almost all to four-year schools, and more than half will go to private colleges.

Gate of Heaven has an adequate curricular package designed to provide its graduates with a reasonable preparation for a four-year college, with more demanding college preparatory classes available for those students who wish to push themselves. The counseling program, however, begins in the ninth grade and offers students a chance to learn about college for the first time; it adds emotional preparation to their college planning framework. Nearly all Gate of Heaven students go to college, although nearly all go within a two- to fifteen-mile radius. Two-thirds of students end up at four-year schools, while one-third go to community colleges.

University High School has a full college preparatory curriculum and a counselor who meets with students at the beginning of their high school careers to ensure that they are in the suitable classes. Students are not encouraged to deviate from their preordained place in the academic hierarchy, although, at a teacher's behest, an academically successful student will be provided with opportunities for enrollment in advanced placement classes. Counseling for specific college choices does not begin until the junior year and assumes that parental knowledge will be passed on to students regarding the difference between public and private, CSU, UC, and community colleges, and other basic information that frames the range of expected student college choices. Half of UHS students enroll in UC and CSU schools across the state, while another third of UHS graduates attend private four-year colleges throughout the country.

Mission Cerrito's curricular advising is loosely coupled (Weick 1976) to its college counseling, with differentiated tracks of college preparatory courses and some advanced placement classes. Placement in the higher tracks is dependent upon two variables: parental/student knowledge and advocacy, or strong junior high school test scores. College counseling at MCHS assumes very little: Mr. Sirotti's booklet offers basic information about the GED, SAT, and ACT exams, as well as about the three public California postsecondary systems, particularly the community college options. Only 15 percent of Mission students focus their aspirations on four-year schools, and that population primarily attends a nearby California State University or a nearby private university. The majority of college-bound Mission Cerrito students (55 percent) attend the three local community colleges.

Organizational Habitus

Habitus, to reiterate, is a common set of subjective perceptions which individuals receive from their immediate environment and which is shared by all members of the same social class. These common perceptions frame individual aspirations. Habitus is both the combination of the objective probabilities and the subjective assessments of the chances for mobility. Thus, in high school environments where students have their college aspirations framed and enabled, I am proposing that organizational habitus is the view of the opportunity structure of American higher education officially presented to all students.

Each of these schools offers four distinct habiti in which college choice decision making occurs: the actual structure and resources of the school devoted to college preparation—timing, availability, and support for college advising—and the normative structure of the high school—an organizational mission that more or less emphasizes college, most explicitly through curricular options; assumptions of students' cultural capital that the offical guidance program can build upon; and counselor role expectations and enactment that display and reinforce the taken-for-granted nature of a subset of the 3,600 U. S. colleges that counselors have first-hand knowledge of and recommend students attend. Each of the actual and normative structural components presents to the students in those schools a particular *organizational habitus,* the impact of a cultural group or social class on an individual's behavior through an intermediate organization, the high school.

Of what use is the concept of organizational habitus? How does it compare to organizational culture or climate? How is organizational habitus different from high-SES culture in general? Bourdieu (1977a; 1977b; 1984) has found that culture supports and co-determines structures, including educational structures, and he suggests looking at the interaction between social structures and a group's habitus. However, his own class reproduction model has an underdeveloped explanation of the dynamics of individual and structure interaction and an underspecification of the link between individual agency and social structures, particularly schools. Organizational habitus shows how high schools' organizational cultures are linked to wider socioeconomic status cultures, how social class operates through high schools to shape students' perceptions of appropriate college choices, thereby affecting patterns of educational attainment, and how individuals and schools mutually shape and reshape one another.

Organizational culture and climate research has failed to link an organization's internal culture to its larger socioeconomic environment (Ouchi and Wilkins 1985). Organizational culture is defined as an organization's underlying values, beliefs, and meanings, and organizational climate refers to the resultant attitudes and behaviors of individuals within the organization. Culture is deeply held, static, and enduring, while climate is the current malleable perceptions and attitudes that are the contemporary manifestations of culture.

The recent empirical use of organizational culture does not capture the complexities of organizational contexts and does not help one understand the social class similarities of schools as much as organizational habitus can. In this context, the *general socioeconomic status culture* would be the value of college degree attainment useful for conversion to occupational, economic, or other capitals. A high school's college-choice *organizational culture* would be its values related to college attendance and any beliefs as to whether students should attend "any" college or only "better" colleges. Since climate refers to the impact of culture on individual behavior, then a school's college choice *organizational climate* would be the institution-specific current patterns of college choices and behaviors that are manifested in one school in a specific historical period. Finally, since organizational habitus is the impact of a cultural group or social class on an individual's behavior, through an intermediate organization, then the college choice *organizational habitus* would be the specific current patterns of college choices and behaviors that are manifested in schools with similar socioeconomic status environments.

The difference between college choice organizational culture, climate, and habitus can be illustrated by the following example. Paloma School has been preparing young women for college since 1907, this is its deeply enduring value or organizational culture. However, the organizational climate has periodically re-structured how Paloma facilitates its graduates' educational futures through the targeting of specific colleges, the structure of its advising operations, recommended application practices, and so on. College admissions environments also shape the culture and climate of these high schools. Paloma and University high schools are shaped by a national, volatile, competitive college admissions environment (McDonough 1994), while Mission Cerrito's and Gate of Heaven's organizational habiti are shaped by local opportunity structures. Thus, the college choice organizational habitus that Paloma has is the same as UHS in terms of tastes for good colleges and for successful admissions managment practices (McDonough 1994), which maximize college opportunity.

Bourdieu (1977b) describes habitus as a set of dispositions that is durable *yet* constructed anew in each generation. How habitus is constructed with each iteration is first through parents or other socializing agents, or what Bourdieu calls "a whole universe of ritual practices and also of discourses, sayings, proverbs" (1977b, p. 167) and second through the material and social environment. Hence, high-socioeconomic-status students value a college education as much in the late twentieth century as they did in 1907, but in times of relatively rapid social change this vision of what is good and how to attain it will be mediated by the objective conditions of the material and social environment, the competition for access to good colleges, and what Paloma and UHS graduates need to do to remain competitive.

The evidence in this chapter supports a claim that a college choice habitus exists and is transmitted to individuals in organizational contexts as well as through families and social class communities. Habitus is a way to generate strategies that are time- and context-specific, "a matrix of perceptions, appreciations, and actions and makes possible the achievement of infinitely diversified tasks." (Bourdieu 1977b) How is the context for college choice decision making in each of these high schools evidence of habitus? Habitus is behavior constrained by practical and strategic considerations, as well as by the demands of the moment. Each of the guidance counselors has constructed norms for behavior and expectations for the students she or he advises. Each counselor makes assessments of the objective probabilities of his or her students' chances for admissions and subjective assessments of those students' chances at happiness or success at various institutions. The counselors offer their assessments to students through handbooks, the array of college representatives they invite to the school, the information packets they keep on hand to pass out to students, and the collective seminars and individual advising sessions.

Individual and community values serve as constraints to any particular habitus, and certainly the counselors are aware of and sensitive to parental demands or expectations for "appropriate" colleges or information. But recall that the central role of habitus is in defining and limiting what is seen by an actor and how it is interpreted. In this case, Paloma displays private college options and not community college information; Gate of Heaven focuses attention on the UC, CSU, and community college options; UHS highlights UC and CSU; and Mission Cerrito spotlights the virtues of preparing for the "real thing" by living at home and brushing up at the community college. At the first three schools then, the information and attitudes conveyed to students result in behavior that predominantly gets students into four-year colleges, while Mission Cerrito's information and expectations channel the majority of students into two-year colleges.

This chapter has examined how schools structure or affect student decision making and has offered evidence that this is done through timing, availability, and support for college advising; organizational mission and curriculum; assumptions of students' college cultural capital; and counselor role expectations and enactment, which creates an organizational worldview that serves to delimit the full universe of possible college choices into a smaller range of manageable colleges that students can and should attend.

CHAPTER FIVE

Families, Friends, and Finances
As Influences

A student's college choice is the result of a complex relationship between individual agency, family cultural capital, and the structure and organization of the school, to which the student adds the influences of friends, the family's financial situation, an after-school job, as well as numerous other influences. The important task of this chapter is to verify the subjective experiences of students, articulate the salient cultural contexts, and discover the sources of dissonance between the culture of students' communities and families in contrast with the culture of the schools.

When considering the myriad influences as a student makes college choices, think of a mobile. For each individual student who is choosing a college, every influence has a different weight and the mobile hangs in a unique way. When the family is silent because of lack of relevant cultural capital, or passive because of competing time demands, then school and friends may be stronger influences than the family. Since students' decision making processes are the focus of this study, this chapter analyzes the variety of ways in which friends, parents, siblings, after-school jobs, and family finances separately and together influence these high school seniors.

Cultural capital is derived from one's social class and provides an individual with resources which, if used effectively, can provide needed advantages in social institutions (Lareau 1989). In this chapter, I offer evidence that parents give their children resources to make their college choices in a variety of ways. Some parents who themselves have attended college remind their daughters of tasks that need attending to, help keep them on schedule, and assist by reading or editing essays and other application materials. Sometimes parents will help their daughters understand that their current SAT score can be enhanced with coaching, or parents will secure the services of a private counselor, either to help the student put together the best application portfolio or to deal with the ever-present stress of

111

today's admissions scene. Other times, parents will pressure their children to attend schools that are out of their reach, given the child's academic achievement.

Other parents will be supportive but not terribly active in their daughters' college searches, while still others will limit their daughters' searches for reasons related to wanting to keep them close to home or to keep the costs down. Some parents who have not attended college and are unaware of the differences in status or even graduation rates of various colleges, limit their daughters to applying only to institutions where they know the "people are more like us."

Since the Paloma and Gate of Heaven students have chosen to go to private schools, this chapter also reveals a story of some families that are consciously acting to manage their children's educational careers to maximize returns on investments. This chapter looks at the relationship between the families and schools as a kind of dialectical "mating" that occurs throughout a student's educational career that works to facilitate certain students attending certain colleges. Also, for the financially advantaged parents of this study, hiring a private counselor is part of the larger strategy to maximize returns on investments.

One cautionary note—many researchers believe that some parents, students, and counselors overestimate the case for any substantial impact of the type of college on an individual's ultimate educational or occupational attainment. In fact, Pascarella and Terrenzini (1991), in their encyclopedic *How College Affects Students,* and Astin (1993), in *What Matters in College,* both suggest that after applying statistical controls for students' characteristics upon entry to college, the choice of one four-year college over another has only minor influences on educational and occupational attainment. However, parents and students are more likely responding to widely covered media stories of average salaries of elite college students, or "street" knowledge in which many people claim to know that elite colleges give their graduates network and opportunity advantages. In fact, a recently completed study by the Consortium on Financing Higher Education,[1] an association of thirty-one of the most selective colleges and universities, showed that ten years after college graduation, 65 percent of those institutions' college graduates had advanced degrees, the vast majority of which were J. D.s, M. D.s, and M. B. A.s. Although this study is classified as proprietary knowledge, parents and students know and act on knowledge like this and are neither sophisticated about, nor ultimately very interested in, researchers' statistical controls.

Choosing a Private High School

As was mentioned in Chapter Three, many parents of Gate of Heaven students chose a Catholic high school for their daughters as a way to keep them from drop-

---

1. Litten, Larry, 1995, personal communication.

ping out, getting pregnant, falling into the wrong crowd, or experimenting with drugs. As Karla Franco's father put it, public high schools are "big and chaotic and uncontrolled, and I didn't think she was ready for that environment." Mrs. Hauptman appreciated the Catholic school approach to discipline, the close communication with parents, and the way that students are prepped academically for college, so Charlene, like her brother before her, "knew what they had to do" in high school to prepare for college and the application process.

For many Paloma parents, choosing a private prep school for their daughters' secondary schooling was explicitly linked to their daughters' comfort, leadership development, or positioning for college. Although the Steins' local public high school was an "excellent academic school," they were worried that Leah "would not do very well at all" socially. Moreover, the Steins compared Paloma to their local high school, a neighboring high school, and University High School and found "it was clear that the worldview at Paloma was quite different . . . We had no idea where Leah would head in four years, but . . . it looked like more would be possible." In addition to identifying Paloma's intimacy, individualized education, curricular flexibility, and remarkable physical facilities, Mrs. Stein appreciated the

> climate, atmosphere . . . the intangibles that have everything to do with what it feels like to go to a school . . . you see a faculty member walk across the quad with their arm around the girl . . . you can just see the closeness of student-faculty contact.

Mr. and Mrs. Stein also were "knocked out" by the fact that at Paloma "two-thirds of the faculty have Ph.D.s" and "half of the class is looking at the top schools in the country." In their search for the right private high school for Leah, the Steins explicitly looked at the college destinations of graduates.

> The proof of the pudding is . . . where the kids go . . . [These destinations] should tell you what you're going to face, in terms of college acceptance and college possibilities . . . The list of who got accepted to what colleges was stunning.

Thus, the Steins enrolled their daughter in a high school that was "inconveniently" located twenty miles away and "frighteningly expensive." Although both parents are practicing psychologists, they candidly described themselves as not "wealthy" and viewed the steep tuition bill as "a big decision," but Paloma "looked so good . . . it was simply a matter of what's best."

For the Harrimans, private schools were a must from the beginning of their daughter's educational career. Mrs. Harriman's strong beliefs about private schools and their individualized attention stem in part from comparing her own Catholic school education to her sister's more painful, public school experience. This deeply affecting outlook was coupled with a conscious concern about the limitations of being a working mother. "I knew I'd always be working . . . I will never have the time to be at the school [or] really monitor things closely." Because of this time constraint, her ever-present strategy was

> I want these kids in an environment where we're paying for that kind of attention. And then I can expect it and I can know that it happens, because that's the modus operandi in a private school, and it just isn't in a public school, and you can't expect it.

Mrs. Harriman also believed that just as her daughter's elementary education had positioned her well for a rigorous, college preparatory secondary education, "then high school should be a good background for college." Moreover, she felt strongly that her daughter should attend an all-girls school to develop her leadership potential. Mrs. Harriman believed attending Paloma would provide Susan with the opportunity "to get a good crack at a really good education that will set her up for the rest of her life."

Choosing a Private College Counselor

> Well, see the thing is, no matter what you do people are going to try to sell themselves and you can't prevent it.
>
> (Rebecca)

The norm for the last decade has been heightened competition among individuals to get into college and, among institutions, to recruit the cream of the high school crop. (Fitzsimmons 1991) This competition impacts not only college admissions practices but also individual applicant behavior. I will now address one college admissions practice of many of today's upper-middle class students and their parents who appear to be following legitimated cultural rules and patterns of activity; that practice is hiring a private counselor.

As a society, we rely on professionals such as doctors, lawyers, and therapists. Thus, what can parents do when their children are facing the first major choice of their lives at a time when parent-child relationships typically are most strained? Parents, who are aware of how complicated college applications have become and who have the resources to do so, seek the help of outside experts. These consultants do the research, advise the parents and students, and relieve some of the pressure. As Mr. Ornstein articulates, parents hand over their trust: "We simply deferred to her. It's as simple as that. If we hire somebody as the professional, I believe that we've got to listen, if it makes sense."

These counselors-for-hire provide help with completing college applications, coaching for SATs, allaying fears, editing essays, and managing peer pressure. Some of these professionals prefer to be called consultants to distinguish their services from psychological counselors (Stickney 1988), while others emphasize the emotional component of their work (Antonoff 1989). A major selling point with parents and students is the ability of these counselors to offer individualized attention. These entrepreneurial educational consultants are estimated to number between 200 to 500 (Krugman and Fuller 1989; Holub 1987; McDonough 1997; Stickney 1988) and are clustered in large cities and more affluent suburbs. Many of these counselors have themselves come from the ranks of high school counselors or college admissions officers.

In this study, three Paloma students—Candy, Judy, and Kimberley—and two University High School students—Sara and Rebecca—employed the services of a private counselor. All knew beforehand about the existence of independent counselors and had only to ask their friends and peers for a referral. Candy was the only student who saw a private counselor on her own initiative; otherwise, the path to private counseling for this sample of students was overwhelmingly determined by the parents. Kimberley and her parents decided to use a private counselor because her parents did not know "what to do" and they were disenchanted with Paloma's guidance program. Rebecca's mother "thought it would be a good idea" to get some help with the college choice process and wanted to give Rebecca a push.

Mrs. Taylor initiated private counseling assistance because she felt Judy needed SAT coaching and help with her emotional well-being: Mrs. Taylor "didn't want this crazy person" on her hands. Mrs. Taylor was dissatisfied with the school counselor who collected draft application essays and then returned them to the students after summer vacation with no feedback.

> You're supposed to come up with six or seven different essays for these
> schools and here was one important one and there was just no help.
> So that's what I thought a college counselor did for you, was help you.
> So maybe I kind of panicked a little, but I don't know how to tell her
> to write a good essay . . . I don't know what they're looking for.

Mr. Ornstein was overwhelmed by the specifics of finding "out in each school how it works" and the need to identify schools where the SATs "will not carry the ball" since his daughter's scores were modest. He and his wife also felt his oldest daughter's college choice process was less than ideal: "We said this time we would do it a better way."

SAT coaching was a major draw and the presenting problem for most of these young women. Judy Taylor began with her private counselor for SAT coaching, while Candy explicitly bought the services of independent counselor Mabel Cross because of what she felt was a "pitiful" discrepancy between her verbal and math scores on the SAT. She felt "math is something that you can . . . work at and manipulate it so that you can get a better grade." Candy believed the private counselor's services were "a package deal" and that she could not say, "I want to do the

SATs and not do the colleges." Her SAT coaching was "wonderful" and it helped increase her math score by more than 100 points.

Candy felt that using one particular counselor was "the trendy thing to do" and at Paloma "certain girls . . . went to her." It seemed taken for granted that a senior would use a private counselor, one woman in particular. As Kimberley put it, "there's a lady around here who helps you . . . apply to schools . . . get organized." Possibly because this counselor had been previously employed at Paloma, her services were widely known to Paloma's students and families.

Candy, however, felt that except for SAT coaching, private counseling was "a mistake." She felt that you should "get from your own school . . . technical things" like how-to information for filling out applications or information about particular schools. She felt private counselors often wanted to get too involved in the student's application preparation. She said she had to keep her counselor at bay, particularly when it came to writing application essays.

> You should write your own essays . . . we would like fight whenever I'd go in, because I didn't want her to look at my stuff, I didn't want her to get her hands on it.

She also felt that having the counselor become too involved would be obvious and a liability in admissions deliberations.

> When the application comes into those schools, if you follow her instructions as she wants you to, the thing would scream private college counseling, which I think would be a very negative thing.

However, Judy Taylor appreciated Mabel's involvement with the essay process because, "I don't like writing essays, and she knows when you have a good essay, and she helps you brainstorm." Aware of the controversy surrounding private counselors, Judy was quick to emphasize that Mabel "never wrote my essay . . . I wouldn't have let her touch it because it's my process."

What role did the private counselor play in Judy's essay development? According to Mrs. Taylor, when Judy was having trouble coming up with an essay topic, she and Mabel discussed what might be appropriate and interesting subjects as well as Judy's accomplishments and awards. Mabel recommended that Judy write an essay that would allow her to speak about an Ivy League institution's book award she had received in her junior year of high school. Judy went to the library and read books on the historical figure after which this award was named. She produced an imaginative essay in which she met this figure and they discussed their common interests. Judy, her mother, and Mabel all felt pleased with the resultant essay. Judy and her mother were especially grateful for Mabel's suggested strategy: first, that Judy find a way to write about the award she had received and second, that she research the man the award was named after to stimulate possible essay topics.

Kimberley, using the same counselor, had a far less satisfactory relationship, but for altogether different reasons. As with school counselors, some students and their independent counselors have personality conflicts. Kimberley felt her private counselor "was a little pushy . . . and I left a couple times crying." Moreover, Mabel's penchant for keeping students on task in the college application process conflicted with Kimberley's being sick with mononucleosis. In Kimberley's words, Mabel kept "bugging" her because she was afraid Kimberley was going to miss the deadlines. Eventually Kimberley's parents terminated the counseling arrangement.

Kimberley, Judy, and Candy made use of both the school counselor and a private counselor for advice on the college choice process. In spite of supplementing Paloma's advising services with a private counselor, both Candy and Kimberley expressed gratitude toward Mrs. Ball for her help as well as some guilt about betraying her. Candy said, "We have a very good college counselor . . . it is sort of a slap in the face to Ms. Ball to be going to a private college counselor." Judy, however, did not try to talk with Mrs. Ball much about her college choice process because "she had a lot of people to deal with" and students had to sign up for appointments. Many students and parents mentioned that having the independent counselor appointment meant they had a specified time where "you go to your Mabel session once a week." In particular, Judy liked "having my appointment just straight for me without having distractions of people walking in." An important difference to Judy between her school and private counselors was that Mabel Cross, in reviewing Judy's potential college choices, "would just tell you seriously whether you had any . . . chance to get in."

The University High School students and parents who used independent counselors were not at all apologetic about doing so. Sara's father bluntly summed up why his family employed the services of a private counselor to help them through the maze of college choice decision making and application "packaging."

> We have no confidence in the school to provide that service. It's as simple as that. We felt that we have somewhat of a problem here with Sara because of her SAT and achievement tests results and . . . we wanted to make sure that she gets to the right schools, and so that was why we decided to be more involved.

In her quest for college counseling to meet her individual needs, Sara spoke to Mr. Dix and Ms. Dean, as well as to her independent counselor. Private counseling was an absolute necessity, given her frustration with Mr. Dix's nearly total reliance on the UC or CSU systems. "I never wanted to go to UC . . . it really irritated me . . . every time you go in there to ask a question, 'Well for the UC scale.'" Sara knew that the personality match between herself and Ms. Dean was not right and felt that the ratio of counselors-to-students mitigated against effective counseling. "I just think they need possibly more than one lady dealing with everything." Sara liked being able to call her private counselor whenever necessary to ask questions "without feeling guilty." Sara was pleased with the counseling connection she and her private consultant made: "It's more like she became my friend so she could understand what I was like so that she could think of schools where I would be happy." Sara needed her spirits boosted and needed encouragement to apply to a range of schools, from safeties to reaches. But what she was most concerned about was the discouragement she got from her school counselors: "'Don't even bother you're not going to get into any of them' . . . just lowers you right away. You can't have that."

Rebecca Feinbaum did not find consulting with a private counselor particularly helpful and spoke with disdain about her counselor. "All she wanted was to give me a . . . list of schools that she knew I would get in." She felt that her private counselor "didn't know me at all . . . didn't have any confidence in me." Rebecca went back to Mrs. Dean and updated her daily about the developments in her college-mating game.

Many students and their parents spoke of the major help provided by the private counselors in organizing the college choice process, especially when they helped seniors find a way to conduct their college choice process in a way that fit into an already busy senior year schedule. Judy's mother said

> what she did really was take the pressure off us to organize it . . . all the information which we don't have without a lot of research . . . then she set it all out . . . with all the deadlines written down, so it became a manageable process that Judy just chipped away, week by week.

Students received organizing tips, SAT information, college summaries, financial aid, and other materials. Their private counselor worked out a master plan with personal schedules for weekly tasks. Parents and students appreciated the private counselors spending time and resources to visit college campuses to make or keep the acquaintance of admissions staff so they were able to provide students with a firsthand perspective about individual campus climates and offerings.

The other major reason cited by parents and students for using a private counselor was to receive help with the emotional burden of the current, high-pressure college choice process. As Candy expressed it, "A lot of girls went . . . out of fear that this whole college thing was out of their control and they needed help." Mrs. Taylor, expressing a parental perspective on the pressures of meeting high school requirements while managing the college choice process, was concerned with Judy's mental health.

> She wasn't sleeping at night and she was crying a lot, just really being under pressure. I said "Honey, please, it's okay. There's a plan for your life . . . all we want you to do is go where you can succeed . . . get in a school where you do well, and that's the whole point. Getting the degree is the whole point, but feeling good about yourself and living through this whole process is even more to the point.

Mr. Ornstein was equally concerned that the application process pressures were dragged out through the entire year as seniors waited for college acceptances. He was particularly concerned about his daughter's physical health and how the stress was "taking its toll, there is no question about it. . . . We reduced it a little bit by taking the advice of the counselor." He saw hiring a private counselor as a foregone cost of protecting his daughter from heightened competition in today's college admissions environment. "It's not cheap. . . . We never thought twice about it, because when it comes to education . . . money is the last consideration."

Independent consultants charge between $30 to $125 per hour and parents usually spend between $400 and $2,500 (Stickney 1988) to help their children define their postsecondary opportunities and select the college of their choice. For parents who have the financial resources and are willing to so invest, college choice assistance costs are not limited to private counselors. *Time* magazine has estimated that with application fees, private counselors, SATs and coaching, college visits, and private tutors, where necessary—all of which were costs incurred by students in this study—the cost of applying to college can run over $3,000.

Available research shows that about 3 percent of all first-time, full-time freshmen use independent counselors (McDonough et al. 1997) and that these student are from upper-middle class homes where families view nonschool-based admissions support services as an absolute necessity in the struggle to guard against losing ground in the status and economic security game. The families in this study felt the need for a counselor who looked beyond the school transcript and the SAT profile, one who saw a student who was capable of more than what the dismissive bottom-line numbers suggested. These families had the luxury of being able to buy the assistance they needed.

Most admissions staff believe private counselors' services do not alter students' ultimate college choice outcome (Krugman and Fuller 1989), although the families felt their private counselors reshaped the outcome by introducing a wider or different range of colleges to consider than what was apparent to the student or high school counselor. Admissions practitioners believe students using consultant services are academically weak, economically advantaged students, but in fact research shows students who use private counselors are economically privileged, have higher SAT scores and high school academic records than the average college-bound student, and, in general, are advice seekers (McDonough et al. 1997). Rebecca Feinbaum offers the student's perspective on leveraging the accumulated advantages of an upper-middle-class background to maximize college choices:

> I've done all the things that you're supposed to do if you want to get the best advantage that you possibly can get. I'm really a prime case of trying to get into the very best, most prestigious school that I possibly can get into, without maybe having the kind of marks that you should have.

Parents want to invest their sizable college tuition dollars wisely, while seniors want a safe space to be able to talk through their fears and anxieties about making their first important decision in an environment of intense competition and pressure. Many parents and students alike are cued in to attending the "right college," and believe that the best investment in college will come from acceptance at a well-known, elite institution. Parents also are aware that going to a selective college increases one's social standing, contacts, and income potential. (Coleman, Rainwater, and McClelland 1978) This knowledge, however tacit, is chilling in suburbia, where downward mobility is dreaded.

Admissions processes often are viewed, in the words of one parent, as "black magic," or as an erratic, chancy game over which neither parents nor students have much control. Parents who applied and went to college in the days when admissions rates were 30 percent to 60 percent doubt their ability to advise their children through this confusing, competitive maze. They often are aware that aside from purchasing a home, choosing a college could well be the largest capital outlay and the most important investment they undertake. This view is reinforced by the popular press, notably the financial advice periodicals. Those same publications report regularly on the rising costs and increased competition at the "better" schools, thereby fueling economic and emotional insecurity about the best protection for the college-bound (*Business Journal-Portland* 1988; Schurenberg 1989; Stickney 1988).

Family Involvement in College Choice Decision Making

In addition to the advantages of being able to buy the services of a private school or counselor, some of these parents can be viewed as fully participating in their childrens' college choice processes, in the areas of encouragement, involvement, and knowledge, such as being so totally involved in college planning that they overwhelmed their daughters. Others, however, took a hands-off approach and were available when needed, while still other parents were virtually or totally absent. As part of their involvement, parents could be more or less supportive of any piece of choosing a college, or of the whole process. By design, this study selected students whose parents had and had not attended college in order to vary parents' knowledge of basic college application processes.

Levels of Involvement

Many students in this study benefited from older siblings' college choice experiences and consequences. Judy Taylor's parents were not involved in their older daughter's college choice process, an experience which turned out to be quite negative for everyone involved. With Judy, her parents "were bound and deter-mined" that both her college selection and overall college experience would be positive.

Judy's mother was attentive to her daughter's emotional well-being in the college application process. She tried to protect Judy by running occasional inter-ference with Judy's father, who pressured his daughter to apply to his elite alma mater. Mrs. Taylor, who was aware of the admissions prospects her daughter faced, admonished her husband for his misplaced hopes and suggested that he himself would not be admitted to his alma mater today. She encouraged her husband to think about their daughter's emotional health.

> You put so much of your heart and effort into these applications, that
> I don't want her to be disappointed. It's beyond being a long shot. Let's
> put our energy into something that's possible for this girl, not set her
> up for a fall.

Mrs. Taylor was always careful to suggest things that Judy should be doing to enhance her college prospects, from using the junior summer "to do something constructive that you can write down on a college application" to being in touch with recent Paloma graduates at colleges that Judy was interested in for "net-working and seeing what people were doing." In fact, Mrs. Taylor was so involved with her daughter's college choice process that she spoke of it as her own: "We fi-nally sat down and said are we going to go for this . . . Look at all the things that it has that we really didn't want." Mrs. Taylor spoke rather poignantly about want-ing to secure the best education for her daughter to protect her future financial well-being. "We always hope that our children will do better than we did, and that they will go one level higher. . . . I just don't know if it's going to be possible any more."

Kimberley Scott's family also was very involved in her college decision mak-ing, with her mother taking a particularly active role and her father and two older sisters being somewhat less involved. With Kimberley's consent, Mrs. Scott actively advised and directed her daughter's thinking and decision making.

Kimberley, who was the third child to attend college, remembered her old-est sister's experience. "My parents didn't really know how to get her involved" [in the college application process]. Thus, the Scotts hired a private counselor, as they did for Kimberley. With each of the prior children, Mrs. Scott said she was

> always looking for a good place . . . was always thinking in the back of
> her mind, "Would Kimberley like that? Well maybe she would." And
> "would that be a good place for Kimberley?"

Mrs. Scott also helped Kimberley sort through her feelings about whether a school would be a good fit. Kimberley described how her mother's opinion sometimes helped change her own outlook.

Maybe it was my mom saying that 'you don't want to go.' Maybe it was just because we just decided that that wasn't so great for my older sister. . . . So I think that that's kind of how we, my mom changed, and I guess I changed too.

But it is clear that Kimberley sought her mother's advice and welcomed it, which helped her identify some important issues, in particular, her mother's perspective on viewing college as a time for geographical experimentation.

My mom used to always say you only have . . . four years to go away, you might as well go away to someplace where you've never been before . . . and experience something totally different from where you live now.

Paloma's "college days" started Leah Stein thinking seriously about specific colleges in her sophomore year, which the Steins felt was "a year quicker than she might have in public schools." As described by Mr. Stein, he and his wife were very involved in Leah's college choice process even though he admitted that "most of it she did herself." However, their involvement took place within limits carefully set and monitored by their daughter. Mrs. Stein was concerned that, as parents, they "not to express a very strong opinion, or it's liable to guarantee that she does the opposite." Mr. Stein unhappily found out that "if you step over the line, you find out real quick." He got "static" when he tried to evaluate Leah's college prospects for himself and borrowed a guide to colleges to see what was possible for Leah.

I thought maybe knowing her interests, that I would pick out a list for her to look at . . . [Leah] gently let us know that we should stuff it.

Leah's list of colleges was something that she and Mrs. Ball developed and according to her dad, Leah "was not too open at all to adding additional schools to the list." Her driving motivation in putting together her list of schools was "a real strong desire not to be refused." However, both of Leah's parents were much more concerned with, as her dad described it, issues related to prestige and the percentage of students who don't graduate.

For me that's one of the few ways that you can begin to get a hint of do people like it. . . . The small Ivy League schools, the best of them have graduation rates . . . in the 90th percentiles. And it absolutely goes almost with the prestige of the school.

Overall, the Steins felt Leah's college choice process was successful but "intense."

Susan Harriman had mixed feelings about her parents' involvement in her college choice process. She felt "all my dad wanted me to do was go to Stanford. He would just nag and nag and nag." She felt burdened by his history.

He got into Stanford and his parents couldn't afford for him to go all the way out to California, he was living in Pennsylvania. . . . He regrets having not gone to Stanford.

Susan said she felt frustrated talking with him because when she wanted "to let him know that I was really worried," he would push again for Stanford. A relatively soft-spoken young woman, Susan found herself exasperated and saying, "Dad, shut up, you don't know a thing about what college applications are like nowadys."

She felt a similar frustration with her mother who also did not understand the pressures from today's admissions context.

She really couldn't take me that seriously. . . . didn't really understand why I was so stressed. . . . I'd get so frustrated trying to sit down and explain to my parents what it is like trying to get yourself into college. They have no concept of what it's like. I feel like there's all this pressure on me to go to a really great school. . . . pressure with all my friends going to great schools.

For her part, Mrs. Harriman was "aware of the intensity" of Susan's senior year. She tried to encourage Susan by commenting about her extensive research and telling her to trust her own judgment. "I was usually just reassuring her that whatever happens, it's going to be fine." Several times when she felt Susan was getting "overly concerned," Mrs. Harriman contacted Susan's teachers who simply told her "this will pass."

Mrs. Harriman described her involvement in Susan's college choice process as letting her daughter take the initiative, then asking "questions about these different schools . . . And we'd say, 'Oh, I didn't know you were interested in that.'" Mrs. Harriman saw her role as that of a "sounding board," asking how one school compared to another.

Candy Whitcomb's parents were supportive, major players through her two-year ordeal of college decision making. She talked with her mother every day about colleges because "my mother is . . . my greatest fan. She's like my support system." When Candy spoke of her college choice process she often would say "we, because my parents are so tied up in this."

Subtly, both parents pushed for their or their extended family members' alma maters. In addition, Candy's mother occasionally took matters into her own hands. When Mrs. Whitcomb was completing and mailing Candy's UC application, she took the liberty to check off UC San Diego and even signed Candy up for a particular major. Mrs. Whitcomb undertook this action even though Candy had not checked off that UC campus and, in fact, had insisted that she did not want to apply there. In relating this story, Candy laughed and was not particularly troubled, seeing this as an innocuous attempt on her mother's part for Candy to have some sure bets in the final choice set.

What did, however, become a major source of "anguish" for Candy was that she became caught up in "this prestige thing, the name of the school." Although she explicitly stated that her parents did not care about prestige and instead were focused on finding a small college where Candy could receive the individual attention she had at Paloma, she did express frustration with them for "encouraging me to apply to these reaches," not being "realistic," and

> they were almost too much, too supportive. I would have rather have them really remove themselves and say, 'This is up to you, here are our guidelines. Financially this is what we can do.'

Candy was aware that she had lost "perspective" and wondered whether her desired schools were what she wanted or, "is this what my mother wants, or is this what the person down the block said the other day." She knew her "mother would say everything I wanted to hear" and she sought out her comfort in what was a uniquely troubling situation—none of her other friends were applying to colleges a second time, nor had their self-esteem been through the "real battering" Candy had experienced in aiming too high for colleges for two years in a row.

What was problematic about the Whitcombs' role in Candy's college choice process was that Candy wanted them to put the brakes on her "self-destructive" behavior.

> I was just torturing myself mentally . . . going through so much anguish, and it's been going on for like months . . . because they weren't saying, 'No you can't.'

Instead, Candy and her mother kept living out their favorite phrase of "keeping options open." In retrospect, Candy felt there had been a high cost in waiting the first year to be accepted off the Princeton waitlist and falling into that same waiting trap again the second year. She said, "there is a point where . . . you will start to lose things."

At Sara Ornstein's invitation, her parents were welcomed to become part of her college choice process because, "I know my mom and dad want me to be happy where I am" and because University High School was so unhelpful. Sara's parents were "furious" with University High School because "nothing was going on . . . for people like me who don't want to go to UC or Cal State." Mr. Ornstein understood that there was no feasible way for the University High School guidance counselor to help Sara with all of the things he thought were important.

> The guidance counselor does not know and cannot know the children in a proper way. . . . he has a certain image of people from his very limited exposure to them and from the written record.

Sara's father was particularly concerned about the limitations of a cumulative grade point average in indicating the kind of steady upward progress that Sara had demonstrated over the course of her high school career: "You will see that from ninth grade on every year it goes up a little bit . . . She has been substantially improving herself all the time." He oftentimes commiserated with his daughter about the lack of "rhyme and reason" in admissions processes, and he tried to be sensitive to his daughter's vulnerability in discussing the whole subject of college admissions during the period from February to April, when she was "tearing her head off." In addition to her parents' involvement and support, Sara's social networks were a valuable resource. She found a private counselor through her neighbor, a learning disabilities counselor, and had her essays read by her best friend's mother, a writing professor.

Rebecca Feinbaum's mother was extremely involved with Rebecca in making college decisions and in setting the framework for thinking about colleges by informing Rebecca that considering a college's reputation is "helpful to you in the future. . . . if you go to a school that has a good reputation, then there are certain 'ins' that you have in the professional world." However, Rebecca often rebelled against her mother's help. Mrs. Feinbaum pushed her daughter to begin the college choice process "way before I wanted to think about" it, which evoked cries of "chill out" and characterizations of her mother as "supportive and nagging." Rebecca also characterized herself as "being rebellious because I knew how important it was to her."

Rebecca alternately felt indebted to her mother, yet resentful about her mother's inferred pressure. "I've done all of this for you, and so now you owe me at least this." In describing the range of mother and daughter dynamics surrounding her college choice process, Rebecca described a time when the tension was so thick it was "one of the worst experiences in our relationship . . . we were screaming at each other constantly." Yet there was also tenderness, sensitivity, and humor, which both mother and daughter appreciated.

> I was really nervous about all these colleges and full of anxiety. I said "Oh Mom, I really want to go to Brown but I don't know if I'll get in. . . . I think I should just go and see a psychic and find out about my life." I mean it was a total joke, a real laugh. . . . And then on my birthday my parents take me to this psychic. And I said, "You're crazy, I don't want to go to a psychic. I was just joking. It was a big old joke." And they said, "No, no, you're going now.". . . This psychic said, "Tell me one wish and keep one wish in your head." And I said, "Well, I wish that I can go to Brown." And she said, "Your wish will be answered." And I asked her again, and I said, "Will I go to Brown University?" And she said "Yes, yes."

When needed, Mrs. Feinbaum marshalled her resources to help Rebecca. She called a relative who was an admissions officer at a private East Coast college who told her about "some places that weren't getting the kinds of applicants that they wanted to get." Oftentimes, because of the numerous adults who were involved in her college choice process, Rebecca felt there was too much adult pressure.

> At this age whenever you go to anything that has to do with a relative or anybody older they always want to find out exactly what you're doing with your life, what colleges are you going to apply to. And you just turn on this sort of automatic mode.

Marilyn Clayton's father was heavily involved in her college application process, and Marilyn felt he was "really pretty forceful about things when he really wants something to be done." The University of Montana was the only school Marilyn was applying to and it also was her father's alma mater. Mr. Clayton, on his own initiative, decided one day to complete Marilyn's Montana application while she was at school: "I was so mad at him. I said, 'Dad, the one school I apply to and you fill out the application.' He's like 'Well, it's no big deal. It just goes in the files.'"

Marilyn admitted that his intentions were good: he was excited that she wanted to go to his alma mater, he was retired and had more time to think about and organize things, and he was positive she would get in, believing it was just a matter of completing and filing the application. Marilyn also understood his emotional need to believe "that he still has some say in my life." Nonetheless, she felt her father's overbearing ways reinforced a "scatterbrained" self-image and left her feeling "mentally deficient" and that she could not "plan her own life." Marilyn's father had done this many times before, sometimes superseding plans and decisions she had made for herself, including her educational experience during her junior summer. Often she felt "awful" for complaining because he arranged for wonderful things, yet it upset her that "there was something I wanted to do so badly and then he like planned something else for me."

Margaret Avalon's parents were fairly involved in her college choice decision making, in particular, there was "a lot of influence from my dad." When she was a child, her student parents modeled college. Early in high school, her dad kept her from straying off the college track. Margaret's parents encouraged her to take a junior college class while in high school, and it was her mother who first planted the seed of her final college destination. However, when Margaret's mother first suggested Mills College, Margaret's response was, "Oh, yuck." This response primarily arose from a normal child rebellion against parental advice. "Sometimes when your mom suggests something you don't want to like it." Margaret obviously reconsidered.

Margaret did struggle with her parents, however, when it came to essay writing. In one essay, she had to write about a major influence on her life. Margaret chose a particularly inspiring teacher, which caused family problems.

> I cried and stuff with my mom, because she felt left out of the essay because I didn't write about her. . . . So I've decided for my Mills essay,

just so my parents know how much [of] an influence they've been on me and how much I appreciate them . . . if I'm in the process of assessing myself and I want to be honest, I need to include them, and I want to.

Both of the Avalons went to San Jose State and felt that "the state college system is not that bad, but she's still not inclined to go there . . . because of peer pressure." However, they both encouraged Margaret to apply to a wide variety of schools. Mr. Avalon, in characterizing Margaret's college choice process, said that she did most of the work. "We have stood strong behind her, giving direction and help as she needed it."

Constance Evan's father and stepmother were not involved at all in her college decision making, although they were generally supportive. Because he had never attended college and knew nothing about the process, Mr. Evans could not offer Constance any advice regarding college preparation, the SATs. He just assumed Constance must be doing whatever she needed to do, whenever she needed to do it. Moreover, Constance's college anxiety was not understood, in fact, Constance's stepmother said, "It has never occurred to me that she wouldn't be accepted . . . she's done well . . . , and seems to have all the right requirements."

Although they never brought up the topic to their daughter, Cindy Lane's parents were happy to discuss her "college decisions and questions" at her request. More specifically, Cindy felt that "they're really open about it and once you get them started on it they don't want to stop." She was convinced that neither of her parents realized "that there is more pressure now than there was when they" went to college. Cindy's father was always available to offer advice and support when Cindy was wrestling with any problem and, with her college choices, he encouraged her to "take everything step by step." Cindy was perfectly content with her parents' level of participation because she saw choosing a college as her first independent decision.

You have to really break away from basing your decisions on what your friends think, your parents want, teachers say, and really start making your own decision, and take what you want from yourself. And if it's wrong, hey, that's okay, you can always change it.

Cathy Ross's parents are not college-educated, yet they want their daughter to attend college so she can "be successful." As Cathy sees it, college is something foreign, since most people she knows are not college-educated. She does not want or expect much out of college and is comfortable with living at home.

I'm so fed up with hearing about college . . . everyone's 'Oh, you have to go to college, you have to do this, you have to do that.' And it's just like 'I'm going to go to State, Mom. Be happy with that.'

Mrs. Ross's involvement in her daughter's college choice process consisted mostly of typing applications. Cathy talked with her parents "a little but not a lot" about her college plans and considerations. Her parents were dramatically different in the ways they encouraged Cathy to approach choosing a college.

> My dad was like really carefree and my mom was like the hectic one, pushing me to do all this stuff.... we never really sat down and talked about it though. It was always my decision ... But we never sat down and said okay, what are you going to major in.

Cathy's parents did not pressure her to go to any particular or type college. She claimed, "It was better for me that way, because then I could do what I want."

Cathy's extended family also was a constant source of encouragement, although they sometimes created conflict. Her aunts and uncles often pressured her about going into business or taking accounting in college. Moreover, Cathy was confused about the payoffs of a college degree because of the experience her uncle had after obtaining his graduate business degree.

> My other uncle ... my brother makes more money than he does. It just hasn't come in for him yet. And my brother hasn't even gone to a state college; he's just going to a JC. It's weird because my brother got breaks.... You have to go to college and all, but you look at this situation: my brother makes more money than this man ... It's sad, because you have to get the breaks. You have to be lucky.

Darla Lopata's family is supportive but not knowledgeable. Her father periodically checked on her college planning and tried to find books that would help her think and learn about different colleges. He occasionally brought her college catalogs and guidebooks that he received from people along his mail route, people who had already experienced the college process.

> He's always 'check them all out, see which ones you like. But the thing is, I always pick ones that were like away, because I always wanted to go away, but I don't think I'm going to go away ... [because of money].

Charlene Hauptman's parents, particularly her mother, were fairly involved in her college decision making process, although they were not too knowledgeable. "They really don't have all the information to tell me." Although she was generally supportive of Charlene's desire to attend college, Mrs. Hauptman "took it for granted that" her daughter wanted to go. But instead of encouraging her daughter's aspirations, Mrs. Hauptman never had to bring it up.

> I never had to say "Well, do you want to go to college.".... There's never really been, "Well I want you to go to college." I've never had to do that. So maybe it is coming from the schools.

Charlene's mother also had a hands-off approach to grades. Although she reviewed every report card with Charlene, Mrs. Hauptman never pushed her daughter because she did not want to turn her off to school. "All I expected my kids to get was a B average."

However Charlene's brother was involved, knowledgeable, and supportive and had extensive conversations with his sister about going to college, specifically to his alma mater. "That's kind of where I plan on going for the time being. . . . he gives me suggestions on how to go about it and what to do when I first get there," said Charlene. Charlene's brother and his wife both have degrees and professional jobs and, according to Mrs. Hauptman, provided the major family input about Charlene's college choice planning. "It was mainly more through him than me."

Mrs. Hauptman has attended the local community college for a number of years, primarily taking art history classes. Her part-time enrollment provided Charlene with a nice exposure to college. Once, when Mrs. Hauptman needed surgery, Charlene sat in on her mother's art class and took notes. Mrs. Hauptman noted that Charlene "enjoyed it and it kind of gave her a little look at what college is."

Mrs. Hauptman perceived her ability to help Charlene as limited. "Sure I've tried . . . but . . . I couldn't help her with anything." However, Mrs. Hauptman always knew to ask if Charlene needed help, including investigating taking Spanish in summer school, when Charlene was concerned about the impact of a low grade on her GPA. In spite of her own lack of college experience, Mrs. Hauptman made herself knowledgeable about what she thought was important for Charlene's college preparation, especially the minimum SAT score that was necessary for State. When Charlene was worried about whether she got enough on her SAT to compensate her grade point average

> I said, "Yeah, you've got enough." She said, "You sure?" I said, "Yes, because I checked it out.". . . I knew exactly what she needed before she did.

Although Charlene took all of the initiative, Mrs. Hauptman was able to help review her application because of her own experience of being a junior college student. Charlene invited her mother to "go over it to make sure she had done it right."

Jacqueline Davis' father has a liberal arts orientation to college. "You can do whatever you want, just get that education, it's the most important thing." Jackie's family was very influential in cultivating in her a "taste" for a liberal education.

Both of Karla Franco's parents are well-educated and were concerned about Karla going to a "good" school. According to Mrs. Franco, "We are trying to figure out where she could get the best education." However, they openly fought about where, which type, and on what continent Karla should attend college. This intense disagreement left Karla feeling she "didn't want to . . . lean on one side too much." Both parents agree the family has had and will probably "always live with one foot in America and one foot in Europe." This bicontinental dilemma left Mrs. Franco believing that Karla should go to an internationally recognized American college or to an Italian university. However, the problem with the latter option is that Karla does not have a clear career direction or major, and in the Italian university system, a student has to declare a major immediately.

There are other issues at the root of Mr. and Mrs. Franco's disagreement. According to Mrs. Franco, the decision about college options was made clear by Mr. Franco's insistence on attending public universities. He would not let his daughter "apply or go" to any private college. Having narrowed Karla's choices to only state universities, Mr. Franco stayed clear of influencing her choice of backup plans in the event that UC-Berkeley did not accept her.

> It's such a tremendous decision I really don't want to influence her. . . .
> She should make her own decision because otherwise later on she's
> going to point a finger at her father and say, 'you made the decision.'

From Mrs. Franco's perspective, after Mr. Franco narrowed the choice to UC-Berkeley, there was little for Karla to do but wait and see if she should act on the community college option, which Karla vehemently opposed, or if she should invent a major in order to enter the Italian university system.

While Samantha Schaeffer was weighing her college options, Mrs. Schaeffer felt excluded and was not consulted. "I've long since decided that I have no influence in this matter." The Schaeffer family's habitus is "education-oriented," which in large part is due to Mrs. Schaeffer being a former teacher as well as a 16-year veteran of the PTA and various school committees. But the Schaeffer college habitus was "the plan. . . . we told the girls that we would help them as much as we could, but they would have to take the first two years at a junior college."

Although Samantha was "running wild" early in high school, it was Samantha who took herself by the hand, changed friends, and starting hanging out with an academically better crowd. Mrs. Schaeffer was pleased when "her grades improved, her choices in classes changed, her objectives changed." In spite of this change in peer orientation, Mrs. Schaeffer insisted that Samantha follow the community college route when her daughter's grades remained mediocre. As Mrs. Schaeffer perceived it, the prospects of Samantha garnering scholarships seemed impossible, thereby leaving only the junior college option.

Edie Tashimi's parents have college degrees and were concerned about Edie choosing a good college. Her parents recommended "UCs in general" and specific campuses that they had heard positive comments about. Mr. and Mrs. Tashimi received a lot of their information about which colleges were "good" from their friends who had children attending various schools. Edie found her parents incredibly supportive and knowledgeable, while they simultaneously encouraged her to make her own choice. Edie did "pick up on the basics" from her older brother.

Lucy Baker's college-educated, professional parents were happy to be involved in helping her plan for college. Lucy's family helped define her possible college choices, based on her grades.

> What we did was we looked at the information that the school had given us, and looked at what her SAT scores were and what her grade point was and where she could fit in. We almost always thought about a public school for her . . . That's what both of us experienced and so. . . . If she wanted to go to a private school, I certainly would be open to talking about it.

Mrs. Baker also felt Lucy should focus on a small school where she could "get more individual attention" and that Lucy needed more academic preparation to be able to handle college workloads. "She doesn't feel as prepared as she would like to be in terms of like her English classes, her writing skills, and those kinds of things." Lucy began to view her CSU possibilities as problematic and to adopt the perspective of her family, friends, and school counselor—that maybe going to the local community college would provide her with the attention she needed to develop her term paper abilities.

Julie Carlson's college-educated, professional parents were supportive of her as she tried to figure out what kind and where the best college might be for her. "I always had the images from my mom and my dad . . . college is the best time of your life . . . you meet your lifelong friends there." From an early age, her father had encouraged her to work hard at her education and to aim for college. Mrs. Carlson helped Julie with her applications and kept Julie on schedule with application deadlines.

Carol Lincoln's parents were not very involved in their daughter's college choice process, although Mrs. Lincoln made some attempts to participate.

> We have been discussing it. We went to the school last year when they had the college night fair. . . . we did talk about which ones that she sort of liked, the ones she might want to go to. She more or less has applied to the colleges that she had her mind set on.

Mrs. Lincoln's preference, however, was that Carol stay at home.

> Course we'd like to have her go some place close by here. There's some good colleges around here. But she wants to venture away. She was pretty set on going away . . . she says she's always lived here and she wants to go someplace else.

Moreover, Mrs. Lincoln was concerned about Carol's lack of explicit career focus. "She doesn't really know what she wants to go into." But as with her overall relationship with her daughter, Mrs. Lincoln was timid and tentative about her ability to influence her daughter's thinking and decisions. "If I see she's going in the wrong direction or something, I'll try to speak up."

Kay Baptiste's parents were generally supportive but not knowledgeable about the college experience. Kay's parents "didn't really push. They've always like let me decide where I wanted to go and what I wanted to do. And they always tried to stand by me." Kay often looked to her father for help and advice. All of the people in Kay's and her parents' circle of friends had jobs such as court reporters and teacher's aides, for which they had community college terminal degrees. Kay's parents' friends sometimes were influential in making minor suggestions to her about college, especially regarding majors and careers. However, their encouragement almost always was geared toward the terminal community college curricula with which they themselves were familiar or from which they had graduated. "A lot of my mom's friends tell me things I should do, give me suggestions."

Geographical Influences

Several areas of parental involvement warrant specific attention because they point out class-based resources or patterns. One area has to do with geographical constraints imposed by self, family, or friends on the area over which students cast their college choice net. The widest views of geography expressed by students in this study were those of Karla Franco and Laura Frescotti, both of whom considered or are attending Italian universities, primarily because of their experience of living in Italy. The other students who seriously considered and now are attending schools outside of California were all from high SES backgrounds: all of the Paloma students, Leah's best friend Sarani Zagreb, and Sara, Rebecca, and Marilyn from University High School.

However, all students who considered or are actually attending colleges away from home articulated a desire to be an appropriate distance from home, which always was explained as being able to come home when lonely, or being able to have one's mother come quickly to visit during an illness. Judy Taylor had the most highly articulated and differentiated sense of geography, which was both freeing and constricting when it came to choosing a college. She "wanted to get out of California"; yet the college had to be within one day's trip, preferably close enough to a major airport and on an air route that would require taking only one plane.

Edie did not think about leaving California because of the weather and distance. Julie Carlson's geographically constrained view of her college opportunities were that she wanted to apply to colleges where she would be in-residence and in-state, while her parents wanted her to be within driving distance. The Avalons wanted Margaret to consider "a school somewhat closer to home" since their older daughter's school is "inconvenient" because it is too far away.

Kimberley Scott talked about wanting someplace "not that far away from home" that was "two hours, maybe a little more than two hours" travel time away so she could come home for the weekend. That distance, whether discussed by Kimberley or other high SES students, is defined by air travel, "even though it's a little . . . extravagant to fly all the way home for a weekend." Students who considered colleges away from home but within California and those who considered colleges across the United States all define distance, not in miles, but in units of time: a couple of hours away from home. However, the high SES students' families have the financial resources to define that time by air transportation, while the other students' families define time by two hours of ground transportation—bus or car. This is not to say all of the families who sent their daughters to colleges outside of California would fly their daughters home for the weekend, as suggested by Kimberley. However, the distance seemed more acceptable because the cost of air transportation to and from school at least once a year or during emergencies did not seem prohibitive.

There were several other ways in which being away from home was made more palatable. One was that students talked about the potential discomforts of being away as mediated by having people they knew in the area, whether they were contemporaries, school chums, family, or family friends. For example, the Avalons' friends in Eugene introduced Margaret to the University of Oregon and made it seem more accessible because she knew people there. In considering the University of Montana, Marilyn felt comforted by having relatives nearby and already having "some friends there" because of the summer program she attended during her junior year.

Students talked about it being "nice" to have friends or family at college in case of an emergency or, as Edie described the benefit of having her brother at her school, "it'd be just kind of security." Several students who considered going away to college were discouraged by their families from considering those options. Mrs. Lincoln was concerned for Carol attending San Diego State because, "I . . . would like for her to have somebody she knows go down there with her. Right now there's not that many people that she knows of." Cathy Ross's parents and brother did not understand why she wanted to go to Sacramento State and ridiculed her and told her that considering colleges "down South" was not good either because it was just trendy.

Although Charlene was glad for the information available at Gate of Heaven's career center and for the counselor's encouragement to go away to school, she acknowledged that it was not enough to make college feel accessible without her family's support. When Charlene wanted to consider colleges where she could be in residence, her brother and his wife incredulously asked, "Why?!" and were not particularly supportive. Mrs. Hauptman was extremely opposed to her daughter going away to college.

> I tried to discourage that because I said . . . what's wrong with San Francisco State? Here she's got her own room and my husband works nights, and I'm never around to bother her . . . this is like you're living by yourself.

Moreover, Mrs. Hauptman explained to Charlene the monetary bargain she would receive if she lived at home, just as her older brother had before her.

> I didn't expect him to give us anything living at home. I wanted him to concentrate on his college education and that's what I try to encourage her. Because I says, "It sounds real good to move out, Charlene," I said "but you're going to have to support yourself."

Mrs. Hauptman conveyed to Charlene that going away to school presented a tougher financial balancing act than did living at home.

For some students, parental encouragement to attend college away from home waivered after the students manifested ambivalence. Julie's mother was "really excited" about Julie going to college away from home and took time off from her own job and graduate education studies to take Julie on college tours. Julie's parents encouraged her to apply to several schools that would allow her to be away from home and to enjoy the full college living experience. When Julie began to waiver about moving away, her parents reconsidered and felt this was the only viable option since Julie was having difficulty in committing her full effort to a college away from home. Mrs. Schaeffer and Mrs. Baker also expressed these same sentiments. Mrs. Baker wanted to be as supportive as possible but Lucy's indecision lead her to believe that Lucy should stay home for another year. "If she had said, 'I definitely want to go away to school, I'm prepared, I'm ready.' There's no question then, I think that's fine, that's showing that she's ready to go."

A final area of concern regarding breaking away from home and community was the impact moving away would have on friendships. Kay Baptiste was not comfortable with her best friend Carol Lincoln going away to school and worried about the impact this would have on their friendship. Kay did not want Carol to leave because it made her feel "kind of weird. All that time you spend with her and then she's going to leave." These two friends are taking altogether different life paths, and Kay feels abandoned because of Carol's decision to move away.

College Visits

Another area where students from high SES backgrounds approached college planning differently from their low SES counterparts was in visits to colleges. Both high- and some low SES students mentioned needing to visit colleges before agreeing to attend. Susan Harriman said, "I could not go to a school that I hadn't visited." Constance Evans expressed her opinion that visiting colleges was an absolutely essential step.

I didn't know anything about the school and about the area . . . I don't think it's a good idea to apply to a college that you haven't visited . . . It's important to feel comfortable where I'm going.

Carol Lincoln's first college visit took place when she was visiting an aunt who lived near Texas A & M and her "aunt pretty much knew where everything was, so we just drove around." Carol's mother described a later visit to San Diego State as more organized because it included a campus and a dorm tour. This description of a college visit is different than any offered by the high SES students of this study. For example, Mrs. Stein had an explicit agenda for how college visits should be structured, which included a tour, an interview, an overnight stay, preferably in a dorm, and a chance to attend a college class. Moreover, she told Leah she wanted to "make sure you have set foot on the campus and gotten some feel for what it's like to be there."

Many of the high SES students spoke of visiting many colleges, sometimes repeatedly. Candy Whitcomb made two separate college trips to the East Coast to look at schools, while Leah spoke about four separate trips: her first was with her brother as he went through his college choice process, the second was with a friend, the third was with her mother, and the fourth was alone. The trip with her mother included scheduled tours provided by admissions office representatives.

Many high SES students asked rather specific questions of interviewers or campus tour leaders in an attempt to get a feel for that college's particular environment. Susan Harriman spoke about her concerns coming from an all-girls high school and feeling that "it was really important for me to find a place where women were valued as much as men." Thus, she asked the interviewer

If I was in a class with a teacher who didn't really seem interested in what I was saying . . . if I really felt like I was kind of up against a wall, how would that be addressed?

Sometimes students felt they had to keep their parents from shortchanging these college visits. Sara Ornstein had a problem with her father wanting to make one trip over a long weekend to minimize time away from work. She informed him, "We're going to look, we're not going to just rush through." Margaret's visit to Mills College, even though the school is less than fifty miles away, included attending a class, staying in a dorm overnight, and

they had a program and they had an interview, and I . . . really really liked the interview. It was like, just a nice conversation. The woman seemed to have good insights into who I was.

College visits were such a routine expectation at both Paloma and University High Schools that these schools, unlike Gate of Heaven and Mission Cerrito, had policies about authorized absences for college visits. However, several Paloma students felt pressured not to miss school time and some spoke about teachers pressuring students to not let those absences affect their particular classes. Mrs. Stein expressed dissatisfaction with Paloma about expectations regarding college visits. Although Paloma allowed students to take several days of excused absence for college visits

> you still have to make up your work. So the amount of pressure goes
> up two or three notches, and it's also at the time when you're doing
> applications, and so you don't have any extra time.

Karla Franco's father was the only parent who expressed a jaded view about organized college visits: "They simply sit you down and tell you about the history . . . but they don't really tell you . . . the standing of the school in the academic environment."

Some parents, like Mrs. Stein, felt strongly that their daughters should make an additional round of college visits when making their final decisions in order to have some basis for figuring out where they would feel most comfortable and get the most out of their college years. The Steins also had an interesting perspective on empowering their daughter during these college visits. They clearly wanted to do as much as they could for their daughter and to figure out and provide "the most that we could make happen." Several of the high SES parents spoke of using a business resource to keep down the costs of this part of the college choice process. The Steins said: "We had a ticket available from some frequent flyer stuff, so it wasn't going to cost us a thousand bucks to send her" back East for her final trip. Maybe more importantly, as many of her high SES counterparts have done, Leah already had experience traveling by herself, therefore, her parents "weren't really worried about" her being on her own. Mr. Stein knew that Leah's solo trip boosted her ego. "Everybody that she ran into . . . was absolutely astounded that there was a kid from California who was there by herself." Mrs. Stein also knew that the last college visit had a most important feature.

> Taking this trip by herself to Maine and seeing what it would be like
> to be alone that far away from home was part of what was important
> about the trip. And that's why she wanted to do it by herself.

In the traditional sociological and psychological literature, working-class youth are perceived as not being as developed as their middle class peers, because they do not set out on their own, are too dependent on family and peer groups, and do not question authority (Steinitz and Solomon 1986). What I hope I have shown is some evidence that individuals make sense or meaning from lived experience; therefore, class can only be understood in context. In this perspective on geography and college visits, the high SES students conducted themselves differently from their low SES peers because they had prior experiences that enabled them to know how to behave differently. Leah had traveled by herself before, so when it came time for her solo college visit she knew how to handle herself. She had a context for traveling and meeting new people, based on traveling with her parents. Also, she had a budding habitus for experiencing new worlds by herself or with peers because of her earlier college visit with her friend Darcy and because of her solo travels.

Susan was able to ask questions of campus authorities regarding how she would be treated as a female student because she had been taught and encouraged to consider herself a bright, entitled thinker while at Paloma. She looked for a context, or a habitus, in college that she had been shown and came to expect from her high school habitus.

Friends

For the high SES students, there is a seamless quality to their world: friends, family, and school personnel all expect that everyone goes to college. Mrs. Harriman spoke of the reinforcing nature of Susan's family, school, and friends: "She was in an environment where everybody was going to go to college." Susan herself spoke at length about the pervasiveness of the college information and assistance from her friends and school.

> There are people at Paloma who if they had been in a public school they wouldn't be going to college, there's just no way. . . . You find out so much just sitting around the senior lounge during one period . . . Just word of mouth and sisters and brothers who have gone to college and we just all constantly were sharing the information about college and it was like the center of our minds. . . . Miss Ball is like an unending resource. . . . we'd go up and talk to her four periods out of six during the day. And the teachers at Paloma are really always open, talking to you about college and are interested in where you are going, supportive, willing to help you write an essay and spend time with you after school. . . . that's part of what you pay for going to a private school. Especially, I think about the recommendations . . . to have people who know me really well. When I was deferred, to have my U. S. history teacher mail them one of my essays and write me a recommendation without even mentioning to me . . . that sort of personalized attention.

Marilyn, a student at University High School, spoke about how college attendance is something "you just kind of assume . . . especially around here in this kind of community." Some of the girls even spoke of their boyfriends as being reinforcing college influences: Karla's boyfriend gave her "incentive," while Margaret's boyfriend was a positive influence because "seeing him going to college, and I wanted to go too. Not necessarily the same one, but just that he does."

Rebecca discussed a distinct habitus about college in her life. She said she came to reflect on her community's and high school's expectations that everyone should attend college after noting the contrast with a neighboring community with high high school dropout rates and low college expectations. She did volunteer work in that community and came to believe that if college expectations are not "set up within the school community, then it isn't cool, and if it isn't cool, then kids don't pass it on."

Yet, as Rebecca noticed, not all communities nor all people within all communities are geared toward college attendance. Several students at Mission Cerrito talked about their friends not having college expectations, especially Kay Baptiste's. For Kay, there is only her best friend Carol Lincoln and "a boy, somebody I know, that's going to go to junior college for a year." Moreover, Kay's college-bound friends don't talk much with her about their college plans or share much in the way of information: "Just this one guy . . . talks alot to me about it. . . . that's pretty much the kind of people that talk to me about it." For Kay, being without a strong school influence, not having many college-bound friends, òr not having parents who are immersed in a college-aware network of friends, the influences on her college aspirations are sparse and intermittent.

For Charlene Hauptman, there was little support for going away to college among her circle of friends at Gate of Heaven and her family. Once, while shopping with her mother, they ran into a Gate of Heaven alum who had tried going away to college. This young woman was now living at home and told Charlene, "It sounds really great, but the next semester I was home. I got so homesick, you don't think you will . . . but you will."

For Carol Lincoln, having friends who were college-bound, and specifically those who were actually considering CSU schools, enlarged her perception of college opportunities beyond what some friends, Mission Cerrito, and her family habitus suggested. "I was going to go a junior college. And then everybody was applying [to CSUs], so I thought, I'll apply just for the heck of it."

Samantha, aware that if she wanted to attend college she would need the support of like-minded peers, actively switched friends in the tenth grade. Samantha's new friends were "all going to a four-year" and she had a close-up view of their situations and pressures. Sometimes though, watching them was "depressing because I wanted to go so much." It caused some internal conflict for Samantha to know her friends were going to places she would like to be able to consider but could not.

For Julie Carlson, there is a certain continuity to her friends' college expectations that is reassuring. Most have reduced their expectations from CSU schools to junior colleges. One friend has always been anomalous—Caroline, one of the highest-achieving students at Mission Cerrito. Yet Julie and her other friends accept Caroline's difference. They all have known for a while that she will have different college expectations and they support her in taking the road less-traveled. "All along she's been straight A's . . . It's like we all kind of accept that as, well, that's what Caroline was going to do."

Edie Tashimi has a stratified friendship structure. "Most of my friends are going to different colleges, or some of them are just staying around here and going to junior colleges." These two sets of friends bring with them two sets of behavioral expectations.

> With my school friends, we don't really talk about college too much. . . . But with my other friends that go to different schools, we talk about it, about what it's going to be like.

Edie was not the only one who had to manage two worlds of friendship. Karla Franco spoke of having to carefully manage college conversations with some of her Gate of Heaven friends.

> I don't really want to talk to them too much about it . . . mostly because I don't want to like be, "Oh yeah, I applied blah blah blah" and then I get rejected everywhere . . . Most of them didn't even apply to UCs, so I don't want to like rub it in. On both sides it's better not to.

On the other hand, having friends focused on college attendance and applying to the same colleges often caused just as many problems as those experienced by Edie and Karla. Rebecca Feinbaum had a major conflict in that she did not always feel supported by her friends, all of whom were in the same situation, sometimes competing for the same limited number of elite college spots.

> This friend knows that I want to go to Brown . . . I get the feeling that she thinks that her other friend, who also applied to Brown, really deserves to go to Brown more than I do. So I was just feeling really insecure.

Rebecca said that at some points during her senior year, when the fear of rejections hit its zenith, she and her fellow students begin to limit their college conversations with each other, which "made it a weird dynamic." Susan Harriman spoke of similar dynamics at Paloma and gave an example of how she responded to those students who had heard about their acceptances before she did. "You're just sort of like, 'Great, I'm really happy for you.' But what am I going to do." Cindy Lane's friends did not pressure her but they did question her about how she felt about only applying to two schools: "Is that going to be okay? What if you don't get in?" She tried not to get defensive and consoled herself with not having to write endless essays and spend huge sums of money on application fees.

Marilyn's friends helped her deal with the emotions of being at odds with the general high-status, college orientation of University High School: "My friends aren't the kind of people who would put any judgement on what you want to do . . . that's the main thing that helps me." Her father was concerned about how "excessive" the peer environment at University High School was, with so much emphasis on selective schools that students were not really deciding, but following the herd, and more importantly, for those students who made "different" college choices "they seem to have to feel embarrassed."

Finances

High SES Students and College Finances

There were major differences between the high and low SES students in when and how much family finances influenced their college choices, apart from purchasing a private secondary education or a private counselor. For many of the high SES students, money was not an issue in choosing a college, as was the case for Susan, Judy, Kimberley, Edie, Cindy, Rebecca, Sara, and Marilyn. As Susan explained,

> it didn't play a factor at all. I didn't even know what the colleges
> cost . . . my parents can afford to send me to a four-year private school,
> they told me that from the outset that I could go wherever I wanted.

Susan did ask her parents occasionally, "Can we afford it?" Her father would reassure her that "we will manage it." He said obviously they were interested in how much the tuition was going to be, but that Susan should not let it be her "deciding factor." Mrs. Harriman encouraged her daughter to check into scholarships, which Susan did not very seriously explore. However, as Mrs. Harriman noted,

> we've been paying tuition all of her life . . . it's kind of become a way
> of life with us . . . our attitude was we knew we would be paying col-
> lege tuition someplace and so we just sort of factored it in.

Many of these students did not consider the tuition when selecting colleges, even though they knew UCs were extremely inexpensive compared to the other schools to which they were applying. Judy claimed she was not really interested in attending a UC and that her chances of getting into one were a long shot, but applied because her parents found the tuition appealing. In spite of this acknowledgement, UCs were never a serious consideration for Judy or her parents.

Rebecca and some of the other high SES students—Susan, Kimberley, Marilyn, and Sara—often discussed their relative privilege of not having cost considerations. "It's lucky that I don't have to worry about the financial aspect of colleges, which a lot of people . . . do." As Sara went on to explain, it was not that her family was so wealthy that money was not something they needed to think about. Rather, "my parents really want what's best for me, and somehow or other they'll come up with whatever it takes, just because that's the way they are." Sara's family is even filling out a financial aid form for some of the schools, but she is convinced that "we're not going to get it . . . I'd love to get it, but I don't think I will." Moreover, Sara's attitude about the financial aid forms is to leave it up to her father. "I'd really like to stay out of it . . . he's the one who said don't worry about it in the first place."

For some other high SES students, like Susan, there was occasional guilt about her privilege as she thought about other students who might not have the same opportunities. She described a United Negro College Fund television advertisement that made her feel uneasy: "There's that boy and he really wants to go to college and he really looks like he deserves it and he can't, he can't afford it." Susan and a friend discussed this advertisement and their good fortunes. The two girls discussed whether each deserved the advantages they had, in light of this young man's situation, and wondered "how many of those kids that are out there who really wanted to go to Harvard and can't go, can't afford it? It's like so twisted."

For some of the relatively advantaged high SES students there was guilt about the cost of the colleges they were considering. According to her father, Leah was concerned about whether they could afford a private school. "The difference is going to be on the order of $12,000 a year" and especially, "how could you inflict all this monetary damage on your parents when you had an acceptance at UC Berkeley." Mr. Stein spent several days convincing her that it was okay with them for her "to make the decision to spend more money and go to a small school, that she had earned the privilege to make that decision by suffering through Paloma."

Rebecca, who was aware of her privilege yet comfortable with choosing a good school regardless of the cost, offered an interesting counter perspective.

> I think oh gee, if I go to UC Santa Cruz, then there'll be a lot of money waiting for me when I get out of school. Because that's the deal . . . But I have no problem using that money for going to school. I'm fortunate.

Moreover, Marilyn felt that, regardless of what she might want, her attendance at college was a priority for her parents. "It always seemed more important to them that I go to college," therefore she assumed it was something they wanted "to pay for."

For four of the high SES students—Candy, Margaret, Karla, Margaret, and Lucy—money was a serious consideration, although the way the tension around this issue was played out was different in each case. For Candy, in the UCLA versus Barnard choice, "money especially was the major issue." However, it really began the year before in the Princeton debacle. When there was a chance that Candy would get into such a prestigious place as Princeton, her parents were just as "tangled up" in feeding her status desires as she was. They expressed their intention to support her regardless of her decision, even when Candy felt "it's not even realistic financially." She sometimes resented being "the responsible one saying 'this is not realistic.'" Moreover, she saw their responses to her overshot expectations as being born of their own feelings of inadequacy.

They tend to want to be able to do as much as they can . . . It's hard
for them to say we can't afford this. They don't want to say it. It's just
in the past years, we've been having financial difficulties.

For Karla Franco, money defined her college choices. Although her father
was willing to pay for college, private schools were just not "worth the money."
Mrs. Franco was upset that Karla's choices were entirely constrained by her husband's unwillingness to pay for a private education. "He wins because, of course,
Karla cannot go to a private school because he's not paying the tuition." Mrs.
Franco said that if Stanford had been a possibility, Mr. Franco would have done
whatever it would have taken because he claimed that would be "an investment,
just like buying a rare piece of art." For Mr. Franco, finances, institutional prestige,
and achievement were in a delicate balance.

For Margaret Avalon, money was an issue from the beginning of considering schools. She had a sophisticated knowledge of the state financial aid system and
the availability of money, especially for private colleges. This knowledge came from
having an older sister already in college. Margaret said,

I need to stay in California for monetary reasons if I'm going to go to
a private school. There's absolutely no way without any money from
the state, for me to go to a private school out-of-state.

Her father also was aware of what Margaret needed to do for financial aid and he
wanted to be sure his daughter understood her financial obligations before making her final decision. In particular, he wanted her to understand the long-term,
loan "obligations she will have." Mr. Avalon also said that he and his wife would
"help her some."

For Lucy Baker, money was a consideration insofar as she could only afford
to attend a state university. Luckily, that was her desire. Her parents were happy to
pay for her college expenses and conveyed that financial backing to her. Mrs. Baker
said that starting in elementary school they "began putting away money for her."
Julie Carlson's parents had a similar attitude about assuming all of the responsibility for financing Julie's college education. "Finances would all be taken care of by
my dad." However, Julie was grateful and never assumed her parents had to help.
Her gratitude sounded distinctly different from her Paloma and UHS counterparts: "It's been offered to me . . . like on a silver platter and I feel very fortunate
to have parents that would consider it so important that they'd pay for everything."

Low SES Students and College Finances

Almost all of the low SES students assumed they should take the initiative to figure out how to finance their college educations, although their parents might be

able (but not expected) to help. The best example of how this played out was in the responses of Constance Evans and her dad to the question of how Constance would pay for college. Constance said, "I don't know," while her father said, "Good question." Mr. Evans did not give another answer or elaborate on the possibilities, while Constance went on to talk about how she would work with the high school counselor and her parents "to figure that out."

The low SES students' language about financial responsibility was reversed from that of the high SES students'. The low SES students were responsible for financing college, while their parents (or sometimes extended family networks) "helped out." Jacqueline Davis stated that her family would "help out a lot" with the costs of college, especially her grandmother, who already had paid for Jacqueline's Gate of Heaven tuition.

Cathy Ross did not want to be a burden on her parents, even though her father tried to encourage her to not "worry about the money . . . go where you want to go." Although they agreed to pay for a major portion of her college tuition, Cathy said "that's a lot for them to put out." Cathy has class-bound conceptions of when her adulthood starts. With her parents paying for college "it'd be like I'd be living off them . . . I know I'm a burden on them now, but I'm still in high school." Cathy felt that she should be financially responsible for herself after high school, yet she also knew that being solely financially responsible meant that she would be forced to forego attending a CSU and instead attend a community college, the cheaper, albeit less desirable, alternative: "Why pay $700 or whatever it is at State when you could pay $50 at City and get general ed there? I mean, even though it's not as good a school."

One low SES student, Darla Lopata, stands out as saying she did not worry much about how she would finance college because she knew her parents were going to pay for it. However, Darla only looked at California State Universities, decided not to be in-residence at college, and considered UC schools too expensive. "My parents said if I really wanted to go to a UC they can come up with it." Because her parents were paying for college, Darla felt strongly motivated to choose a cheaper alternative than UCs or private colleges: "It'd be cheaper on my parents." However, Darla also felt relieved that college would be cheaper than her Catholic high school. For Darla, a college education was not out of her range of financial possibilities, but living in the dorms was.

Charlene Hauptman also had money for college, an inheritance from her grandmother specifically "for the actual college and not really the dorm and everything else." In Charlene's overall college choice scheme, money was "an influence." According to her mother, there never was any real consideration of anything other than living at home and going to State because of "the cost." Besides, Mrs. Hauptman felt "there's nothing wrong with State." Mrs. Hauptman equated UC Berkeley and Stanford in terms of how equally out-of-reach those colleges were in relation to Charlene's finances. She then went on to advise Charlene: "If you want to go to a bigger [in name or stature] college, you're going to have to pay the rest. We've paid for your education through this point."

Constance's stepmother's concern was that Constance should not be expected to pay for school totally through loans because that would mean an onerous repayment burden.

> I'm wondering like how much the average state college student is going to pay out for four years of college on loans. . . . you can't fund your college . . . with all that at the end of it. It has to be real supplementary, I wouldn't want to owe more than 25 percent of the entire cost. . . . I wouldn't want to see her get out of college with a $10,000 loan or more.

This concern grew partially out of her own difficult experience in repaying her loans after dropping out of college and not making a decent salary.

Carol Lincoln assumed she would finance college by using financial aid. She filled out the many required financial aid forms and assumed that somehow she would work it out. Like Constance's stepmother, Mrs. Lincoln was concerned.

> Well, I'm a little bit worried. I will be curious to see how much the financial aid will help out. I'm not too sure how much or what. I'm hoping that we get a little something to sort of help us to get her down there. I know we can get her down there the first year.

Mrs. Lincoln's remarks underscore an important point for many of these low SES families: when faced with uncertainty in the long-term financial outlook for college, just take it one step at a time.

Financial aid often was spoken of in similar terms by both the high and low SES families. Mrs. Schaeffer was vehemently opposed to jumping through the financial aid hoops with Samantha after her older daughter's negative experience: "We do not qualify for financial aid . . . You just can't get it, and you give them every detail of your life. I went to the meetings, and I looked at the papers." Darla Lopata assumed her family would not qualify for financial aid but worked with her father in completing the forms, just as Sara Ornstein and Candy Whitcomb had. Jacqueline decided that since she was going to live at home, financial aid was "not necessary."

Interestingly, Charlene Hauptman felt it was wrong for her to consider applying for financial aid because her parents were "going to help out" and because she did not feel that "it was necessary. . . . I figure why should I use it when someone else who really could use it. It's there for someone else . . . I've never even really looked into it."

All of the low SES students stated that they expected to work in college—Constance, Darla, Cathy, Carol, Samantha, Charlene, Kay, and Jacqueline. As Constance said, "I know I'll work when I got to college. I couldn't see not working."

However, several mothers—Mrs. Lincoln, Mrs. Schaeffer, Mrs. Hauptman, and Mrs. Evans—expressed concerns about their daughters managing the college workload and part-time jobs. Constance's stepmother also was concerned about the prospects of finding employment in a small college town "because there are just so many students flooding in there."

For Mrs. Hauptman, a college job was a necessity and Charlene's high school job was not only a known quantity but more importantly, already compatible with school. A good job was yet another reason why going away to school was too risky. "At San Diego State you have to go down there, you're going to have to work. . . . this job she has now, she can regulate her hours with her schooling."

Job As Influence

For some students in this study, the jobs they held while in high school played a part in their college choice decision making process. Charlene's part-time job in high school factored into her final round of college choice decision making. According to her own and her mother's descriptions, she had a job with a decent future that allowed her to attend State and save money by living at home. Charlene said her job is

> a reason why I want to stay here right now . . . I'm learning a lot . . . that kind of influences me to stay here. . . . I could get a job if I went away, but I don't think one that I enjoy this much.

Moreover, Charlene was influenced by her mother's view of the occupational opportunity structure, which was a direct result of her mother's work history with the phone company. Mrs. Hauptman had worked her way up to "a top job" as supervisor.

> To get a good job, you've got to get your degree. When I left the phone company . . . they were not promoting through the ranks like they did when I started. . . . if you don't have your degree in your big companies now . . . you're not going to get a top job.

Mrs. Hauptman encouraged Charlene to focus on the concrete, available steps in getting from high school to a career. Charlene's after-school job was an immediate link to a college major.

> I told her to go for . . . business administration because she's got that little job after school now at the hospital . . . what she fell into is just such a great opportunity for her because they're teaching her the computer.

She sees Charlene's career opportunities through the limited lenses of her own, tempered by the jobs her son and daughter-in-law were able to secure at a major computer and public utility company by having college degrees. For Mrs. Haupt-man, "good" jobs are in management or supervisory positions at large companies.

Like Charlene, Cathy Ross of Gate of Heaven also factored her high school job into her college choice decision making because "I know that I need to work and go to school." One of the reasons she chose to attend locally was because she had gotten a job "in a lawyer's office . . . and I can work my schedule around school." Although several of the high SES students did hold jobs while in high school, none were attributable to the influence of the college choice process. Of all of the high SES students, Judy was the only one who specifically said she would be "willing to get a job" while in college.

Conclusions

This chapter looked at how both low SES and high SES students' parents enlarged or constrained their children's view about their particular piece of the college opportunity structure and how they secured the necessary resources. High SES families bought a private secondary school education or the assistance of a private counselor when they perceived the need.

This chapter also reviewed students' connections to their families and communities and how it affected the distance they considered when going to college, including moving away from home. I presented evidence that high and low SES students' views differed about whether or not they should stay close to the home and community during their college years. The low SES students' feelings about neighborhood and loyalty to friends sometimes combined with their perceptions about geographical constraints to delimit the area over which they cast their college choice net. Low SES students and parents also expressed the belief that if students did not know what they wanted to major in or focus on for a career, then the most appropriate step would be for students to first attend a local junior college.

I provided evidence that all students were concerned with remaining close enough to home to be able to get home quickly or have their mothers come to visit them at school, if necessary. Students talked about wanting to be no more than two hours away from home, however the family's resources allowed low SES students to define that distance by ground travel time, while high SES students defined it by air travel time.

This chapter also discussed the seamless nature of the high SES students' world: friends, families, and school almost always fit together perfectly to focus the students' aspirations on going to four-year colleges, hopefully the best their achievements would allow. For the low SES students, there often were conflicts or challenges. Some students had to weigh their dream aspirations against the realities of their high school's academic preparation. Others had to maintain friendships where different college expectations meant beginning the process of managing being different, while others had to balance delicate financial constraints with needed family emotional support.

How and where cost considerations came into play in the college selection process varied for students from high and low SES backgrounds. I presented evidence that high SES students defer to their parents on this issue. All of the high SES students in this study simply assumed expenses were something their parents "would handle" once acceptances were in hand and that parents would tell them if they were considering colleges out of their price range. The low SES students, at least implicitly, considered costs initially in defining a range of institutions to which they would apply, such as only applying to state schools. Explicitly, however, the low SES students said cost was something "they would work out later." They were aware of financial aid, although some often felt it was useless to apply because people they knew "never got aid." Most importantly, students considered the cost of college to be their responsibility, although many parents expressed a willingness to financially help their daughters.

CHAPTER SIX

College Choice in a
Cultural Context

Findings

This book has shown the myriad ways in which students navigate through the process of choosing a college: from considering a range of appropriate colleges to gathering information on those schools under consideration to making a decision. Students make college choices in the context of implicit and explicit messages from their social and organizational networks. Sometimes the cultural context of the students' communities, schools, and families are in agreement, and sometimes they are not.

To return to the image of a mobile presented in Chapter Five, the students in this study differ in how they weigh different factors in the college choice process; thus, the mobile shifts and hangs in many different ways. For some students in this study, the family, in effect, was silent. Carol Lincoln's parents provide one example of this. They felt they did not know much about college and had little of value to contribute to their daughter's decision. In the framework of this book, they lacked the cultural capital relevant to college choice.

From Carol's point of view, not only was her parents' participation limited, but she felt equally let down by her school. Her poor course counseling in junior high school left her without needed high school science courses and consequently left her having to enroll in remedial classes in her freshman year of college. Her college counselor offered little help in her decision making, other than telling her that the two schools she was interested in were "pretty" campuses near the beach.

Carol's friends were the factors in her mobile that carried the most weight. Carol serendipitously decided to apply to a California State University because some of her high school friends were applying. Both Carol and her friends chose a less well-known route to college, something other than her high school's well-worn path to the local community colleges. As Carol articulated it, she decided on this choice after she watched her friends apply; she herself applied "just for the heck of it."

This college choice process is not the economist's rational choice model of a world with perfect information, nor is it a policy maker's model of informed consumer choice accounting for cost and comfort considerations. It is a teenager left to her own devices in making what she called a "spur of the moment" decision. This spontaneous action was similar to many of Carol's college preparatory actions: studying for the SATs consisted of buying a book two days before the exam and practicing "a little."

Some might ask, "What's wrong with this approach? Carol is attending a decent college." Chapter One provided evidence that where one attends college affects one's chances of getting the bachelor's degree, as well as other educational and occupational attainment, while Chapter Five discussed the evidence that controlling for students' input characteristics at four-year colleges showed little differences in outcomes. However, many of the high SES parents in this study believe and act on cultural capital and habitus—that certain colleges are "helpful to you in the future" and provide "ins" in one's later professional world. Moreover, there are differences among specific institutions, even if there are no differences in types of institutions. At Carol's college, only 30 percent of entering freshmen graduate.

Not all college-bound students face equal choices if they start out with different family and school resources that enable or constrain their educational and occupational mobility possibilities. These differential resources contribute to the persistence and reproduction of a social-class-based stratified system of postsecondary opportunity that thwarts meritocratic ideals.

The students from Paloma and Gate of Heaven had counselors who were able to offer more resources and time than counselors at the other two high schools. Moreover, Paloma students' parents had first-hand college information that they brought to bear on their daughters' choice processes, and they have other relevant cultural capital. For example, Mr. Ornstein knew his daughter's SAT scores (which were comparable to Carol's) could be improved through formal coaching, and he hired a private counselor to help identify schools at which those SAT scores would not be an admissions hindrance.

In other students' college choice decision making processes, parents, regardless of whether they possessed the relevant cultural capital, were relatively passive because of their competing time demands. Susan Harriman's parents, although involved somewhat, left much of the college choice decision making process up to their daughter, which made Susan, her friends, and Paloma School more influential pieces of her college choice mobile. Mrs. Harriman bought private school resources and attention and counted on Susan's home, school, and friendship circles to be mutually reinforcing regarding college aspirations. Nonetheless, Susan felt relatively misunderstood and unsupported by her parents throughout her college choice process.

Lareau (1989) notes that cultural capital, effectively used, provides needed advantages to individuals in their interactions with social institutions. This study documents that cultural capital also confers needed advantages in making the transitions between social institutions by further advantaging those students who have and use family, financial, and network capital to supplement their organizational habitus in trying to maximize their educational choices and eventual returns on investment.

Families and schools are in a mutually influencing process that affects individual student outcomes. Some families have consciously chosen to enhance their daughters' educations by placing them in private high schools or hiring tutors or private counselors. Other parents move to certain neighborhoods to place their children in better school districts. Still other families do not have conscious, educational game plans, and instead react to their children's opportunities based on what school personnel say is possible given their children's demonstrated achievement.

Students' values also enter into the picture. Every student filters her college options through the lenses of her academic achievement, her economic circumstances, her field of vision, and her values. Given these ability, economic, and value constraints, a student eventually narrows down the 3,600 colleges and universities to a piece of the opportunity structure that she believes is within her grasp. This personal schema, including known options and preferences, is the synthesis of what Bourdieu (1977b) calls the objective probabilities and subjective assessments of an individual's chances for mobility.

Although an individual develops her own personally synthesized aspirations, college-bound students of relatively the same academic achievement and similar social class backgrounds make remarkably similar college choices. And those choices are qualitatively different from the choices made by relatively equal-ability students from different social class backgrounds. It is not a coincidence that individuals from the same social class come to relatively similar aspirational schemata. The patterns of students' aspirations in this study were shaped by the class context of the communities, families, and schools in which these students lived their daily lives. These class-based patterns stand in stark contrast to traditional aspiration or expectation research that assumes an individual-level analysis.

The world of choosing a college is much more complex and different than either functionalist or policy maker frameworks suggest. Functionalist educational attainment theory posits that abilities and achievements determine aspirations and subsequent attainment. In this view, college-bound individuals locate their place in the academic hierarchy by matching their prior achievements with appropriate openings. Traditional policy making assumes the same structure of opportunity. The California Master Plan for Higher Education specifies different opportunities for different segments of the college-going population:

- the top 12 percent of California's high school graduates are eligible for University of California campuses,
- the California State University is available to the top one-third of California's high school graduates, and
- the community college system is open to all high school graduates.

In elaborating on Bourdieu's work, I have introduced the concept of "entitlement": students believe they are entitled to a particular kind of collegiate education based on their family's and/or high school's habitus. Class socialization precedes and significantly shapes the formation of aspirations—students develop college plans based on their families' and communities' values and assessments of appropriate goals.

Paloma students felt entitled to the best education they could secure: private when available, or the best public education as a backup. University High School students were, for the most part, from the same geographic and social class communities as Paloma students and felt entitled to at least the best public education and certainly the best private education they could afford. Gate of Heaven students felt entitled to a generic notion of college and whatever was available locally, while Mission Cerrito students felt entitled to the local community colleges.

Class-based patterns of aspirations are a joint product of family and school influences. When families who can afford it choose to send their daughters to private schools like Paloma, they are buying college preparatory services, as well as peace of mind from the perceived problems at public high schools. Other families, like some at University High School, make the most of the college guidance capacity of their daughters' public school environment. Most high SES families in this study knew better than their low SES counterparts how, when, and why they should interact with the school about their daughters' college choice processes. The high SES families had the cultural capital to be aware of nonschool-based admissions management services (McDonough 1994) such as SAT tutoring and private counselors and had the financial resources to then make it possible to purchase those services to supplement their existing family and school resources.

Paloma's college preparatory efforts were comprehensive, proactive, and nurturing. Gate of Heaven's college counseling program also was proactive, providing information and attempting to engage students in exercises designed to stretch their conceptions of appropriate college choices. Gate of Heaven's support for college planning was multi-level and used teachers, students, alumni, computers, and counselors to inform and encourage students.

University High School's counselor conveyed basic and necessary information to large numbers of students about the most popular college choices, but left the college choice decision making process to individual students or their families and could not help students who wanted to consider anomolous choices. Mission Cerrito initiated its college counseling when students were in the final lap of their college choice race—senior year. Students made their choices without much assistance from the school, except for school mailings and bulletins that assumed the best option was community college.

Each of these schools offered different organizational environments for college choice decision making in terms of

1. the actual structure and resources of the school devoted to college preparation—timing, availability, and support for college advising; and
2. the normative structure of the high school

   - an organizational mission which more or less emphasizes college, most explicitly through curricular options;
   - assumptions of students' cultural capital that the offical guidance program can and did build upon; and
   - counselor role expectations and enactment that display and reinforce the taken-for-granted nature of a subset of the 3,600 U. S. colleges that counselors have firsthand knowledge of and recommend that students attend.

Each of these organizational environment features presented to the students in those schools a particular organizational habitus, the impact of a cultural group or social class on an individual's behavior through an intermediate organization. These organizational habiti presented different views of the college opportunity structure and thus framed and enabled students' college aspirations. Organizational habitus demonstrates how high schools' organizational cultures are linked to wider socioeconomic status cultures, how social class operates through high schools to shape students' perceptions of appropriate college choices, thereby affecting patterns of educational attainment, and how individuals and schools mutually shape and reshape each other.

Each of the guidance counselors constructed norms for behavior and expectations for students making assessments of the objective probabilities of individual students and each school's average student's chances for college admissions. The counselors offered their assessments to students through handbooks, the array of college representatives they invited to the school, the information packets they kept on hand to pass out to students, and through the collective seminars and individual advisement sessions. The counselors were aware of and some were sensitive to parental demands or expectations for "appropriate" colleges or information. However, the central role of habitus is in defining and limiting what is seen by an actor and how it is interpreted. For Paloma students, cost was not perceived as a big factor, geography was unlimited, and current academic achievement was manipulable. For University High School students, cost was a modest factor, geography was somewhat unlimited, and achievement often was viewed as subject to enhancement much the same as Paloma students viewed it.

For Gate of Heaven students, cost was a substantial factor, achievement was a modest limitation, and geography was cast in narrow and local terms when considering schools twenty-five to fifty miles away, but most often when attending colleges within five to fifteen miles of their homes. For these Catholic school students and their parents, a private high school education was a hedge against "bad" public high schools and minimal protection against drugs and teen pregnancy. However, public colleges were seen as providing a more-than-sufficient and cost-effective education. For Mission Cerrito students, cost, achievement, and geographical distance were substantial factors. Most of these students did not see their high school preparation as adequate and focused their college sights primarily on nearby junior colleges. The local community colleges, which were some of the best in the state, were viewed by these students and their families as a good investment, a way to "try out" college, and to "sharpen their limited academic skills" in a safe, familiar environment. Even though 55 percent of Mission Cerrito college-bound students went on to attend two-year community colleges, there still was a stigma attached to these colleges.

College admissions environments also shaped the organizational structure and culture of high schools as they related to college guidance. Paloma and University High Schools' organizational habiti were influenced by a national, volatile, competitive college admissions environment that was highly stressful and competitive. These students also lived in a community that was focused on prestige. Mission Cerrito and Gate of Heaven's organizational habiti were shaped by a local opportunity structure and limited family financial resources. Consistent with the research literature, the low SES students looked for low-cost colleges and tight vocational linkages in their educational programs.

At all four schools, students looked at colleges with some concept of habitus, although never calling it that. Some students looked for colleges that matched some aspect of their high school habitus, such as the same supportive environment that had nurtured them during high school. Other students looked for a college habitus that contrasted with their high school experience or was consistent with their own personal values or personalities.

Parents also enabled or constrained their daughters' views of the college opportunity structure, with regard to what were feasible costs, how far from home was appropriate, and whether college was something you entered, or left, with clear career expectations. High SES students' worlds had a seamless quality, while deciding on college was characterized by conflict and challenge for low SES students. Low SES students considered cost in identifying a range of affordable institutions, and these students assumed that the burden of paying for college was theirs. The high SES students usually deferred to their parents on the issue of defining a financially acceptable range of college choices and assumed that the major burden of paying for college lay with their parents.

Enrollment and competition dynamics in the college admissions environment played an enormous role in the process of choosing a college for many of the high SES students in this study. This current method of applying to college is full of uncertainty and heightened anxiety. Many high SES, college-bound students engage in a highly rationalized, managed application process, often employing professional assistance. I described a whole range of new, nonschool-based admissions support services, especially the use of private counselors and characterized students' use of these support services as admissions management behaviors that respond to the heightened admissions competition resulting from colleges implementing marketing and enrollment management practices. Students' admissions management behaviors are individual, class, and organizational responses to a changed, uncertain environment.

Implications

Of what concern is and what conclusions can be drawn from a California study regarding wider populations of college-bound individuals? First, California enrolls 14 percent of all U. S. postsecondary students (Snyder and Hoffman 1995), so in and of itself it is worth understanding how, within a single sizable component of the higher-education opportunity structure, individuals perceive and act on their options. Most states, and certainly the U. S. system in the aggregate, do not have such a highly stratified structure for higher education as does California. However, this book's insights into the college choice processes of its students and their families are instructive to future parents, policy makers, high school counselors, and college admissions officers in and out of California. What is most important is that this study has used naturalistic inquiry to understand how individuals make sense of and move through their social and organizational worlds. Both the findings reported here, and qualitative methods in general, have much to add to understanding and conceptualizing college choice and therefore to understanding the dynamics of college access today.

Through this research, I found that individuals' cultural capital is evident in a sense of "entitlement": students believe they are entitled to a particular kind of collegiate education based on their family's habitus or class status and organize their college searches around a range of acceptable institutions. Paloma students only perceived college opportunities within "the same ten schools, with the Ivy's and all that." University High School students' felt entitled to UC campuses, with elite private colleges as "reaches" and CSU campuses as "safeties." Gate of Heaven girls often found it hard, in an implicit cost-benefit analysis, to justify CSU over community colleges. Finally, Mission Cerrito students most often went to community colleges and those who felt entitled to more, most often went to local CSU campuses and the local private university.

Moreover, high school context plays a significant role in shaping student tastes for particular types of postsecondary institutions. This study demonstrated how high schools' organizational arrangements and processes and the linkages between high schools and colleges help define and mediate individuals' achievements and aspirations.

This study also showed that the cognitive constraints on decision making that bound students' rationality are coupled with individual and organizational cultural and affective premises and satisficing behaviors. Students' college choice alternatives often were influenced by their geographical location, social network, and high school stimuli, as well as by their anticipated college goals and consequences. Moreover, within single high schools, the organizational evoking mechanism—the college guidance operation—had a differential impact on students from different class backgrounds. Individual student behavior in each of these high schools was influenced by the flow and content of college information and the school's explicit expectations that highlighted or downplayed specific options. Assumptions about how familiar students were with basic college information, curriculum prerequisites, and specialized college choice vocabularies had different impacts on students' who did not met or who exceeded those expected levels of knowledge.

Habitus exists not only in families and communities but also in *organizational contexts*. Organizational habitus is a way to understand schools' roles in reproducing social inequalities. Organizational habitus refers to the impact of a social class culture on individual behavior through an intermediate organization, in this case, the high school. These high schools were nested in social class communities that powerfully shaped the specific, current patterns of college choice options highlighted and downplayed by each school, which was reinforced or challenged by the habitus of family and friends. Organizational habitus made possible individual decisions by bounding the search parameters: different schools offered different views of the college opportunity structure.

Organizational habitus is distinct from organizational culture, climate, context, and structure and brings social class back into organizational analyses by showing

- how organizational habitus similarities exist across the upper-middle class communities of Paloma and University High School, and the working-class communities of Mission Cerrito and Gate of Heaven;
- how differences exist between upper-middle class and working-class high schools' organizational habitis; and
- how high schools' internal organizational cultures and habiti are shaped by their larger socioeconomic environment.

Current organizational culture research does not capture the social class complexities of organizational contexts and does not clarify why particular types of high schools produce regular patterns of college outcomes. This study demonstrates the need to reassess equity in college choice and reorient policies to increase students' cultural capital and to reexamine school contexts for equity.

There are implications for policy, practice, research, and theory in these findings. A major implication of this study is the need to redefine equal opportunity in a way that accounts for the cultural dimension of individual opportunity. Clearly, individual students in this study did not always have equal opportunities in fact.

Policy: Cultural and Organizational Equality of Opportunity

In some cases, the schools provided different and unequal resources that enabled different outcomes. In other cases, the parents of these students gave their daughters' financial or cognitive resources to make their college choices. In still other cases, when the school or the family had reached its limits in assisting the college-bound daughter, the family paid for the services of a private counselor.

Scholars and policy makers need to continue to address issues of ability and finances in access to college. However, this study points to both the sociocultural and organizational barriers to the ideal of a truly meritocratic, higher-education opportunity structure. It also highlights the need to discover strategies for expanding cultural and organizational equality of educational opportunities for U. S. high school students. One way to do that would be to increase support for college guidance in public high schools. But, in California and in the rest of the United States, the fiscal outlook for education is likely to remain bleak. What can be done to eliminate or lessen the impact of these organizational and cultural barriers to full equal educational opportunity?

From the perspective of organizational opportunity, better counselor-to-student ratios could offer modest help to college-bound students who lack the family resources to find the "right" college opportunities. For those students whose parents have attended college, more attention to their organizational and counseling needs could be helpful in dealing with the stresses and pressures in much the way that Mrs. Ball does at Paloma. Public high schools could review their college counseling programs to analyze the habitus they are fostering and to make any changes they deem necessary. Public high schools in California need to clearly address their lack of college advising services and to see how they might restructure their current operations, or supplement those operations with new services.

There also is a role for colleges and universities. Admissions offices not only need to rethink their outreach to low SES students, but need to rethink how they might de-escalate the uncertainty and competition for many high SES students. Teacher-educator programs at colleges and universities could also evaluate programs and make future educators aware of the issues presented here and offer suggestions about how they can help future students see the entire college opportunity structure.

Given that the major restructuring of public education necessary for equal opportunity at the organizational level is unlikely any time soon, what else can be done? The corporate sector could be enlisted to help schools provide better college guidance services. Besides corporate grants to improve services, corporate professional staff could work with schools to help students discover a wider range of colleges; students could be matched with mentors who could tell them about a full range of college opportunities.

Colleges and universities could launch a major media campaign targeted to inform not only students but also their parents about the whole range of colleges across the country. The campaign should be aimed to reach junior high and early high school students so they can enroll in the appropriate classes and begin the long process of becoming emotionally adjusted to either going away to college or going to a college "where people are different." This type of media campaign would work best if good consumer information like graduation rates (or transfer rates for community colleges) were part of the message. However, this idea is likely to be met with serious resistance on the part of colleges with low graduation or transfer rates.

Theory and Scholarship

At the level of theory and scholarship, there are implications for scholars conducting status attainment and school climate research, as well as organizational theory and interpretative social science. Scholars concerned with equity in college access should consider how to best study how and why students make decisions about which colleges to attend. I have proposed the extension of Bourdieu's concept of habitus to the organization. Organizational habitus is the impact of a cultural group or social class on an individual's behavior through an intermediate organization and family habitus that is reasonable or rational behavior in context. This study has attempted to show how organizational habitus makes individual decisions possible by bounding the search parameters. Depending on the family resources of the individual student, this organizational habitus reinforces or challenges the habitus of family and friends.

Class-based patterns of organizational habitus cut across individual schools, albeit with slight variations. Future research with a larger sample of schools might specify the general dimensions of school organizational habitus that vary by social class and aim to measure their effects, independent of family variables. Future ethnographic research might explore, in more depth or across more contexts, the social class norms that produce similar organizational context effects and how that influences outcomes and reproduces social inequalities (Anyon 1980).

Future quantitative research should more thoroughly investigate organizational contexts. With specification and operationalization of the indicators of organizational habitus, future researchers might employ multi-level modeling techniques such as Hierarchical Linear Modeling (HLM) to address the equity implications of different types of organizational habiti.

Research about organizational habitus can extend one's understanding of the impact of high school counselors on college-bound students, especially in the case of first-generation college-bound students. Counselors can have an impact on students either through the one-on-one advising situation or, more likely, in the organizational conditions they create for college counseling and planning. For example, Constance Evans who attended University High School and was from a low SES family, found the counselor, the school's "Four-Year Plan," and her peers' assistance invaluable. Her school and friends filled in the gaps resulting from her family's lack of college resources by informing her about PSATs, insisting that she visit campuses before choosing a final destination, and advising and supporting her through the resources of her school's career center.

The data in this study identify the social class and organizational context patterns of a small sample of young women's college application processes. These patterns should be tested with different research populations: males, other racial and ethnic categories, and the highest- and lowest-ability students. One study already has used a quantitative analysis to demonstrate a habitus for African American college-bound students, in deciding between historically black and predominantly white colleges (McDonough, Antonio, and Trent 1997). Extending the research base and assumedly the understanding of organizational or cultural habitus would help policy makers, scholars, and administrators address issues of equality of access in general, as well as increase the flow of low income students and students of color into the academic pipeline.

This study contributes to an emerging sociological tradition of integrating studies of status groups and organizations. Karabel (1984) conducted a historical study of three elite universities and their admissions processes as a case of organizational self-interest. David Karen (1990) examined the organizational context of selective university admissions processes and demonstrated the ways in which meritocratic and class-based factors influence admissions. This project extends that work by demonstrating the dialectical mating of family and school resources in status and educational attainment.

The construct of organizational habitus developed in this study might be extended to research in other organizational contexts. However, this construct may be relevant only to organizations that are in the business of status transmission or educational certification. Future research could test the generalizability of organizational habitus. For example, it could be included and tested in Useem and Karabel's (1986) model of corporate mobility. Such research might discover the diverse habiti of distinctive subpopulations of classes and organizations. The research would have to address questions of specificity: In what kinds of organizations and where or when in all organizations is habitus evident?

Although I offer conclusions and suggestions here about the college choice decision-making process, the framework of cultural capital and habitus also can be applied to studies about how individuals choose either proprietary schools or enter the workforce. Work regarding internal labor markets (ILMs) has shown that occupational information, opportunities, and mobility are structured by different occupations, industries, and organizational arrangements (Doeringer and Piore 1971). This line of research also has shown that there are many job ladders and that individuals progress up the ladder on which they begin. I have shown similar differential structuring of information, opportunity, and mobility in the educational organizations I studied. Future research could extend this line of inquiry to examine other high schools and analyze, in general, if high schools provide entry points on particular educational opportunity ladders in the same way ILMs set a person on a particular corporate track.

This book could have implications for the conceptualization and conduct of status attainment research. A useful refinement of status attainment models could include indicators of organizational habitus and high school–college linkages. Furthermore, given this study's findings regarding bounded rationality, more attention to the role of perceptions is called for and future status attainment models might be expanded to include students' perceived options, independent of aspirations. The status attainment model's focus on individual-level effects has obscured the organizational level effects that channel individual action. Future research needs to make visible schools' roles in channelling and shaping certain repertoires of college choice behaviors.

There also are implications for qualitative research. Qualitative and quantitative researchers need to work together more closely and learn from each others' research. More ethnographic, small-scale studies are needed about school contexts to understand the formation, maintenance, and effects of school and college habiti.

What also needs to be better understood is inter-institutional linkages, such as the one between high schools and colleges. Scholars need to direct their attention to the implications of public high schools' virtual divestment of college guidance. Moreover, they need to study the inter-institutional linkages between families and schools (Anyon 1980; Lareau 1989).

I have examined the process individuals go through in choosing a college. Also identified were the patterns of social class influences on the resources individuals have at their disposal to make these college choices. Clearly, this study is limited because it is a small sample of California students from four high schools, students who made their choices constrained by a highly stratified, public postsecondary educational system. However, the decision-making process and its influences are important across other contexts. The California public education system may present particular patterns of variation in aspirational schemata, but further research will show that the choice process is, in essence, similar in other states. This is a likely result of the strong social class effects shown here that are present even in states where the system of public higher education is not so stratified.

This research has demonstrated that the specific choice of any single individual, illuminating or noteworthy though it may be, is not the only important part of this story. The choice process students go through and the set of outcomes students, their peers, families, and schools define as acceptable also are a main point. The social class and financial abilities of each of these students affected the resources they had at their disposal to make choices about where to go to college, as it does for every student facing these and other kinds of social mobility decisions.

The schools, peers, families, and communities all influenced these college-bound seniors by shaping their range of aspirations, the ways in which they made their final choices, and what they defined as the college education they were entitled to have. It is this influence and shaping of students' aspirations in the context of a class-based sense of entitlement that makes college choice an important issue of educational equity.

This reconceptualization of college admissions problems and prospects reframes issues of educational equity to emphasize the inter-institutional linkages between the secondary and postsecondary educational systems. In conclusion, until the issues of cultural and organizational barriers to equal educational opportunity are addressed, students will perceive many unequal opportunity structures, rather than one to which all will have equal access.

Bibliography

Adelman, Clifford. 1988. "Transfer Rates and the Going Mythologies: A Look at Community College Patterns." *Change* 20: 38–41.

Alba, Richard, and David Lavin. 1981. "Community Colleges and Tracking in Higher Education." *Sociology of Education*. 54:223–247.

Alexander, Karl, and Bruce Eckland. 1975. "Basic Attainment Processes: A Replication and Extension." *Sociology of Education*. 48:457–495.

————. 1977. "High School Context and College Selectivity: Institutional Constraints in Educational Stratification." *Social Forces*. 56:166–188.

Alexander, Karl, and Martha Cook. 1979. "The Motivational Relevance of Educational Plans: Questioning the Conventional Wisdom." *Social Psychology Quarterly*. 43:202–213.

Alwin, D. F., and Otto, L. B. 1977. "Higher School Context Effects on Aspirations." *Sociology of Education*. 50: 259–273.

Antonoff, Steven R. 1989. "Educational Consulting: A Focus for the Profession." *The Journal of College Admissions*. Spring: pp. 27–31.

Anyon, Jean. 1980. "Social Class and the Hidden Curriculum of Work." *Journal of Education*. 162:67–92.

Astin, Alexander. 1993. *What Matters in College: Four Critical Years Revisited*. San Francisco: Jossey Bass.

Barron's. 1986. *Barron's Profiles of American Colleges: Descriptions of the Colleges*. Fifteenth Edition. New York: Barron's Educational Series.

Bernstein, Basil. 1977. "Social Class, Language, and Socialisation." Pp. 511–534 in *Power and Ideology in Education*, edited by J. Karabel and A. H. Halsey. New York: Oxford University Press.

Bishop, John. "The Effect of Public Policies on the Demand for Higher Education." *The Journal of Human Resources*. 12:301–307.

Blau, Peter, and Otis Duncan. 1967. *The American Occupational Structure*. New York: Wiley and Co.

Bourdieu, Pierre. 1977a. "Cultural Reproduction and Social Reproduction." Pp.
    487–511 in *Power and Ideology in Education*, edited by J. Karabel and A. H.
    Halsey. New York: Oxford University Press.
————. 1977b. *Outline of a Theory of Practice*. Translated by Richard Nice. Cam-
    bridge, Great Britain: University Press.
————. 1984. *A Social Critique of the Judgement of Taste*. Translated by Richard Nice.
    Cambridge, MA: Harvard University Press.
Bourdieu, Pierre, and Jean-Claude Passeron. 1977. *Reproduction in Education, Soci-
    ety, Culture*. Beverly Hills, CA: Sage.
Boyle, R. P. 1966. "The Effect of High School on Student Aspirations." *American
    Journal of Sociology*. 71: 628–39.
Brint, Steven, and Jerome Karabel. 1989. *The Diverted Dream: Community Colleges
    and the Promise of Educational Opportunity in America, 1900–1985*. New
    York: Oxford University Press.
Business Journal-Portland. 1988, April 25. "Private Counselors Aid College-Bound
    Teens." *Business Journal-Portland*, p. 1.
California Department of Finance. 1985. *Total and Full-time Enrollment in California In-
    stitutions of Higher Education. Fall 1984*. Sacramento, CA: Dept. of Finance.
Carnegie Commission on Higher Education. 1973. *A Classification of Institutions
    of Higher Education: A Technical Report*. Berkeley, CA: Carnegie Commis-
    sion on Higher Education.
Carnegie Commission on Higher Education. 1977. *Selective Admissions in Higher
    Education*. San Francisco, CA: Jossey-Bass.
Chapman, David W. 1981. "A Model of Student Choice." *Journal of Higher Educa-
    tion*. 52:490–505.
Clark, Burton. 1960. *The Open Door College*. New York: McGraw Hill Publishing
    Co.
————. 1970. *The Distinctive College*. Chicago: Aldine Publishing Co.
Cohen, Arthur M., and Florence Brawer. 1982. *The American Community College*.
    San Francisco, CA: Jossey-Bass.
Coleman, James S. 1987. *Public and Private High Schools: The Impact of Communities*.
    New York: Basic.
Coleman, James S., Thomas Hoffer, and Sally B. Kilgore. 1982. *High School Achieve-
    ment: Public, Catholic, and Private Schools Compared*. New York: Basic.
Coleman, Richard P., L. Rainwater, and K. McClelland. 1978. *Social Standing in
    America: New Dimensions of Class*. New York: Basic.
Coles, Robert. 1977. *Privileged Ones: The Well-Off and the Rich in America*. Volume
    V of Children of Crisis. Boston, MA: Little Brown and Co.
College Board. 1988. *Guide to Secondary Schools*. New York: College Entrance Ex-
    amination Board.
Collins, Randall. 1971. "Functional and Conflict Theories of Educational Stratifi-
    cation." *American Sociological Review*. 36: 1002–1019.

Commission for the Review of the Master Plan for Higher Education. 1987. *The Master Plan Renewed: Unity, Equity, Quality and Efficiency in California Post-secondary Education.* Sacramento, CA: Commission for the Review of the Master Plan for Higher Education.

Cookson, Peter, and Caroline Hodges Persell. 1985. *Preparing for Power: America's Elite Boarding Schools.* New York: Basic.

Corcoran, Robert F. 1977. "How to Go to the College of Your Choice." *Social Policy.* Nov/Dec: pp. 78–81.

Crain, Robert L., and Rita Mahard. 1978. "School Racial Composition and Black College Attendance and Achievement Test Performance." *Sociology of Education.* 51:81–101.

———. 1979. "Reply to Eckland." *Sociology of Education.* 52:125–128.

Davis, Kingsley, and Wilbert Moore. 1945. "Some Principles of Stratification." *American Sociological Review.* 10:242–49.

Dilts, Susan. 1990. *Peterson's Guide to Four-Year Colleges.* Princeton, NJ: Peterson's Guides.

DiMaggio, Paul. 1982. "Cultural Capital and School Success: The Impact of Status Culture Participation on the Grades of U. S. High School Students." *American Sociological Review.* 47:189–201.

DiMaggio, Paul J., and Walter W. Powell. 1983. "The Iron Cage Revisited: Isomorphism and Collective Rationality in Organizational Fields." *American Sociological Review.* 48:147–60.

Doeringer, Peter B., and Michael J. Piore. 1971. *Internal Labor Markets and Manpower Analysis.* Lexington, MA: Heath.

Douglas, William. 1989, February 6. "New Spin on Getting in College: Applicants Hire Private Counselors." *Newsday,* p. 4.

Dunn, Donald H., and Pat Cole. 1987, November 30. "College hunting? Ask someone who majors in it." *Business Week.* P. 157.

Eckland, Bruce K. 1979. "Commentary and Debate." *Sociology of Education.* 52:122–125.

Educational Equity Advisory Council of the California State University. 1986. *Educational Equity in the California State University—Which Way the Future?* Long Beach, CA: Office of the Chancellor.

Erickson, Frederick, and Jeffrey Schultz. 1982. *The Counselor as Gatekeeper: Social Interaction in Interviews.* New York: Academic Press.

Falsey, Barbara, and Barbara Heyns. 1984. "The College Channel: Private and Public Schools Reconsidered." *Sociology of Education.* 57:111–122.

Fiske, Edward. 1989. *Fiske's Guide to Colleges.* New York: Times Book.

Fitzsimmons, William R. 1991, January–February. "Risky Business" *Harvard,* pp. 23–29.

Gardner, John A. 1987. *Transition from High School to Postsecondary Education: Analytic Studies.* Washington, DC: Center for Education Statistics.

Gaskell, J. 1985. "Course Enrollment in the High School: The Perspective of Working-class Females." *Sociology of Education* 58:48–59.

Glaser, B., and A. Strauss. 1967. *The Discovery of Grounded Theory: Strategies for Qualitative Research*. New York: Aldine Publishing Co.

Gottschalk, E. G. 1986, November 7. "Better Odds? Parents Hire Advisers to Help Children Get Into College." *The Wall Street Journal*, p. 33.

Guide to Secondary Schools: California and Hawaii. 1986. NY: College Entrance Examination Board.

Hannaway, Jane. 1987, August–September. "Puzzles, Facts, and Tensions: Inquiry in the Sociology of Education." *Educational Researcher*, pp. 43–45.

Hearn, James C. 1984. "The Relative Roles of Academic, Ascribed, and Socioeconomic Characteristics in College Destinations." *Sociology of Education*. 57:22–30.

———. 1990. "Pathways to Attendance at the Elite Colleges." In *The High Status Track: Studies of Elite Schools and Stratification*, edited by Paul W. Kingston and Lionel S. Lewis. New York: SUNY Press.

———. 1991. "Academic and Nonacademic Influences on the College Destinations of 1980 High School Graduates." *Sociology of Education*. 64:158–71.

Hearn, James C., and Susan Olzak. 1981. "The Role of College Major Departments in the Reproduction of Sexual Inequality." *Sociology of Education*. 54:195–205.

Henry, David D. 1975. *Challenges Past, Challenges Present: An Analysis of American Higher Education Since 1930*. San Francisco, CA: Jossey-Bass.

Holub, Kathy. 1987, April 5. "On Sale This Week: The New, Improved, College Applicant." *San Jose Mercury News-West Magazine*, pp. 14–23.

Hossler, Don, and K. S. Gallagher. 1987. "Studying Student College Choice: A Three-Phase Model and the Implications for Policymakers." *College and University*. 2: 207–221.

Hossler, Don, John Braxton, and Georgia Coopersmith. 1989. "Understanding Student College Choice." In J. C. Smart (ed.) *Higher Education: Handbook of Theory and Research*. Volume V, NY: Agathon Press. Pp. 231–288.

Hotchkiss, Lawrence, and Louise Vetter. 1987. *Outcomes of Career Guidance and Counseling*. Columbus, OH: National Center for Research in Vocational Education.

Jackson, Gregory A. 1980. *Efficiency and Enrollment Modification in Higher Education*. Stanford, CA: Institute for Finance and Governance, Stanford University School of Education.

———. 1982. Public Efficiency and Private Choice in Higher Education." *Educational Evaluation and Policy Analysis*. 4:237–47.

Kanner, Bernice. 1987. "The Admissions Go-Round: Private School Fever." *New York City Child*. (11/23/87).

Kanter, Rosabeth Moss. 1977. *Men and Women of the Corporation*. New York: Basic.

Karabel, Jerome. 1972. "Community Colleges and Social Stratification." *Harvard Educational Review.* 42: 521–62.

———. 1984. "Status Group Struggle, Organizational Interests, and the Limits of Institutional Autonomy: the Transformation of Harvard, Yale, and Princeton, 1918–1940." *Theory and Society.* 13:1–40.

Karabel, Jerome, and Alexander Astin. 1975. "Social Class, Academic Ability, and College Quality." *Social Forces.* 53:381–398.

Karen, David. 1988. "Who Applies Where to College?" Paper presented at the annual meeting of the American Educational Research Association, New Orleans.

———. 1990. "Toward a Political-Organizational Model of Gatekeeping: The Case of Elite Colleges." *Sociology of Education.* 63:227–240.

King, George. 1987. *Conference Report on Minority Attrition and Retention in Higher Education: Strategies for Change.* Sacramento, CA: Assembly Office of Research.

Kingston, Paul W., and Lionel S. Lewis. 1990. *The High Status Track: Studies of Elite Schools and Stratification.* New York: SUNY Press.

Klitgaard, Robert. 1985. *Choosing Elites.* New York: Basic.

Knottnerus, J. David. 1987. "Status Attainment Research and Its Image of Society." *American Sociological Review.* 52: 113–21.

Krugman, Mary K., and John H. Fuller. 1989. "The Independent, Private Counselor." *The Journal of College Admissions.* Spring: 10–19.

Lareau, Annette. 1987. "Social Class and Family-School Relationship: The Importance of Cultural Capital. *Sociology of Education.* 56 (April): pp. 73–85.

———. 1989. *Home Advantage: Social Class and Parental Intervention in Elementary Education.* New York: Falmer Press.

Lefkowitz, Bernard. 1987. *Tough Change: Growing Up On Your Own in America.* New York: Free Press.

Leslie, Larry, and Jonathan Fife. 1974. "The College Student Grant Study: The Enrollment and Attendance Impacts of Student Grant and Scholarship Programs." *Journal of Higher Education.* 45: 651–71.

Levine, Arthur, and Jana Nidiffer. 1995. *Beating the Odds: How the Poor Get to College.* San Francisco: Jossey Bass.

Levine, Daniel O. 1986. *The American College and the Culture of Aspiration, 1915–1940.* Ithaca, NY: Cornell University Press.

Lewis, Lionel S., and Richard A. Wanner. 1979. "Private Schooling and the Status Attainment Process." *Sociology of Education.* 52: 99–112.

Litten, Larry. 1982. "Different strokes in the applicant pool: Some refinements in a model of student college choice." *Journal of Higher Education.* 53: 383–402.

MacLeod, Jay. 1987. *Ain't No Makin It: Leveled Aspirations in a Low-Income Neighborhood.* Boulder, CO: Westview Press.

Manski, Charles F., and David A. Wise. 1983. *College Choice in America*. Massachusetts: Harvard University Press.

March, James, and Herbert Simon. 1958. *Organizations*. New York: John Wiley.

Marshall, Gordon. 1994. *The Concise Oxford Dictionary of Sociology*. New York: Oxford University Press.

McDonough, Patricia M. 1988. "*Class*mates? How Students Prepare for Different College Futures." Paper presented at annual meeting of the American Educational Research Association, New Orleans.

———. 1994. "Buying and selling higher education: The social construction of the college applicant." *Journal of Higher Education*. 65:427–446.

McDonough, Patricia M., Anthony L. Antonio, and James W. Trent. 1997. "Black Students, Black Colleges: An African American College Choice Model." *Journal for a Just and Caring Education*. 3:9–36.

McDonough, P. M., J. Korn, and E. Yamasaki. 1997. "Admissions advantage for sale: Private college counselors and the students who use them." *Review of Higher Education*. 20:297–317.

Meyer, John, John Boli, and George Thomas. 1987. "Ontology and Rationalization in the Western Cultural Account." Pp. 12–40 in *Institutional Structure: Constituting State, Society, and The Individual* edited by G. W. Thomas, J. W. Meyer, F. O. Ramirez, and J. Boli. Beverly Hills, CA: Sage Publications.

Moll, Richard 1985. *The Public Ivys: A Guide to America's Best Public Undergraduate Colleges and Universities*. New York: Penguin Books.

Newsweek. 1989, February 6. "The Alma Mater Derby: High Stakes and High Anxiety at the Top Schools." *Newsweek*, p. 62.

Oakes, Jeannie. 1989. "What Educational Indicators? The Case for Assessing the School Context." *Educational Evaluation and Policy Analysis*. 11:181–199.

Olson, Lorayn, and Rachel Rosenfeld. 1984. "Parents and The Process of Gaining Access to Student Financial Aid." *Journal of Higher Education*. 55:455–480.

Ouchi, William, and A. L. Wilkins. 1985. "Organizational Culture." *Annual Review of Sociology*. 11:457–83.

Pascarella, Ernest, and Patrick Terrenzini. 1991. *How College Affects Students*. San Francisco: Jossey Bass.

Pascarella, E., J. C. Smart, and J. Stoecker. 1989. "College Race and the Early Status Attainment of Black Students." *Journal of Higher Education*. 60:82–107.

Peng, S. S., J. P. Bailey, Jr., and B. K. Eckland. 1977. "Access to Higher Education: Results from the National Longitudinal Study of the High School Class of 1972." *Educational Researcher*. 6:3–7.

Perrow, Charles. 1979. *Complex Organizations: A Critical Essay*. Chicago, IL: Scott Foresman.

Persell, Caroline Hodges, Sophia Catsambis, and Peter Cookson. 1992. "Differential Asset Conversion: Class and Gendered Pathways to Selective Colleges." *Sociology of Education*. 65: 208–225.

Presley, Jennifer. 1980. *Selection and Stratification in Graduate Education*. Stanford, CA: Stanford University dissertation. Unpublished.

Reitzes, Donald C., and Elizabeth Mutran. 1980. "Significant Others and Self-Conceptions: Factors Influencing Educational Expectations and Academic Performance." *Sociology of Education.* 53:21–32.

Riesman, David. 1980. *On Higher Education: The Academic Enterprise in an Era of Rising Student Consumerism*. San Francisco: Jossey-Bass.

Robertson, Larry. 1989. *Organizational Adaptation to Environmental Change: A Study of College Admissions*. Stanford, CA: Stanford University dissertation.

Rosenbaum, James E. 1980. "Track Misperceptions and Frustrated College Plans: An Analysis of the Effects of Tracks and Track Perceptions in the NLS." *Sociology of Education.* 53:74–88.

Schurenberg, Eric. 1989, May. "The Agony of College Admissions." *Money Magazine*, pp. 142–56.

Scott, W. Richard. 1992. *Organizations: Rational, Natural, and Open Systems*. Third Edition. Englewood Cliffs, NJ: Prentice Hall.

Sewell, William. 1971. "Inequality of Opportunity for Higher Education." *American Sociology Review.* 36:793–809.

Sewell, William, R. Hauser, and D. Featherman. 1976. *Schooling and Achievement in American Society*. New York: Academic Press.

Simon, Herbert. 1957. *Administrative Behavior*. (2nd ed.) New York: Macmillan (1st ed. 1945).

Smart, J. C., and E. T. Pascarella. 1986. "Socioeconomic Achievements of Former College Students." *Journal of Higher Education.* 57:529–49.

Snyder, Thomas D. 1987. *Digest of Education Statistics*. Washington, DC: Center for Education Statistics.

Snyder, Thomas D., and Charlene M. Hoffman. 1995. *Digest of Education Statistics*. Washington, DC: National Center for Education Statistics.

Spies, Richard R. 1978. *The Effect of Rising Costs on College Choice: A Study of the Application Decision of High-Ability Students*. New York: College Entrance Examination Board.

St. John, Edward. 1990. "Price Response in Enrollment Decisions: An Analysis of the High School and Beyond Sophomore Cohort." *Research in Higher Education.* 31: 161–76.

Steinitz, Victoria A., and Ellen Solomon. 1986. *Starting Out: Class and Community in the Lives of Working Class Youth*. Philadelphia, PA: Temple University Press.

Stickney, John. 1988, June. "Guides to the Admissions Maze." *Money*, pp. 127–138.

Thomas, Gail E. 1979. "The Influence of Ascription, Achievement, and Educational Expectations on Black-White Postsecondary Enrollment." *The Sociological Quarterly.* 20:209–222.

———. 1980. "Race and Sex Differences and Similarities in the Process of College Entry." *Higher Education.* 9:179–202.

Thomas, Gail E., Karl Alexander, and Bruce Eckland. 1979. "Access to Higher Education: The Importance of Race, Sex, Social Class, and Academic Credentials." *School Review*, pp.133–156.

Time Magazine. 1988, December, 19. "Welcome to Madison Avenue U." *Time Magazine*, pp. 75–76.

Trow, Martin A. 1984, "The Analysis of Status." Pp. 132–64 in *Perspectives on Higher Education: Eight Disciplinary and Comparative Views*, edited by Burton R. Clark. Berkeley, California: University of California Press.

Tumin, M. 1953. "Some Principles of Stratification: A Critical Analysis." *American Sociological Review*. 18:387–393.

Turner, Ralph H. 1960. "Sponsored and Contest Mobility and the School System." *American Sociological Review*. 6:855–867.

Useem, Michael, and Jerome Karabel. 1986. "Pathways to Top Corporate Management." *American Sociological Review*. 51:184–200.

Velez, William. 1985. "Finishing College: The Effects of College Type." *Sociology of Education*. 58:191–200.

Wall, Edward B. 1982. *How We Do It: Student Selection at the Nation's Most Prestigious Colleges*. Fairfax, VA: Octameron Associates.

Weber, Max. [1920] 1978. *Economy and Society*. Berkeley, CA: University of California Press.

Weick, Karl E. 1976. "Educational Organizations as Loosely Coupled Systems." *Administrative Science Quarterly*. 21:1–19.

Winerip, Michael. 1987. "The Hardest Thing You'll Ever Have To Write." *The New York Times*, p. 38. New York: Times Publications.

———. 1984, November 18. "Hot Colleges: And How They Get That Way." *The New York Times Magazine*, p. 68. New York: Times Publications.

Zemsky, Robert, and Penney Oedel. *The Structure of College Choice*. New York: College Entrance Examination Board, 1983.

Index

LaVergne, TN USA
27 January 2011
214219LV00005B/256/A